PEOPLE AND PLACES

A Rainbow Book

Margaret Mead

PEOPLE
AND PLACES

ILLUSTRATED BY

W. T. Mars and Jan Fairservis

AND WITH PHOTOGRAPHS

WORLD PUBLISHING
TIMES MIRROR
NEW YORK

PUBLISHED BY THE WORLD PUBLISHING COMPANY

PUBLISHED SIMULTANEOUSLY IN CANADA

BY NELSON, FOSTER & SCOTT LTD.

1972 PRINTING

LIBRARY OF CONGRESS CATALOG CARD NUMBER: 59–11544

ISBN 0–529–04617–2 (TRADE EDITION)

ISBN 0–529–04674–1 (LIBRARY EDITION)

PRINTED IN THE UNITED STATES OF AMERICA

WORLD PUBLISHING
TIMES MIRROR

PHOTO ACKNOWLEDGMENTS

The author and The World Publishing Company herewith thank the following individuals and institutions whose co-operation has made possible the preparation of *People and Places.*

All possible care has been taken to trace the ownership of every picture included and to make full acknowledgment for its use. If any errors have accidentally occurred, they will be corrected in subsequent editions provided notification is sent to the publisher.

p. 70 (Galileo's telescope)	Alinari Photo
p. 64, p. 81 (Brazil native), p. 82 (New Guinea native), p. 209, p. 210, p. 238, p. 239	Courtesy of the American Museum of Natural History
p. 24, p. 177, p. 207	Gregory Bateson
p. 91	Bell Telephone Laboratories
p. 186	Jane Belo, for *Balinese Children's Drawing* (Overdruk Uit Djåwå, #5, 6; 17e Jaargang, 1937)
p. 83 (Kenya doctor)	British Information Services
p. 293	Emil Brunner from PIX, Inc.
p. 179	Buffalo Museum of Science
p. 82 (Yugoslav)	Paul Byers
p. 182, p. 208, p. 219, p. 220, p. 221, p. 301, p. 302 (Bali)	Ken Heyman
p. 72	Istituto Poligrafico dello Stato (for drawing), courtesy of Collections, IBM Corporation
p. 300	Levitt and Sons, Inc.
p. 187, p. 191, p. 193, p. 195, p. 196, p. 198, p. 200	Macmillan & Co., Ltd., London, and Sir Arthur Evans, for *The Palace of Minos* (3 vols., 1921–30)
p. 176	Courtesy of Colin McPhee
p. 87, p. 90	Courtesy of Margaret Mead
p. 34, p. 35	Courtesy of the Metropolitan Museum of Art Egyptian Expedition Rogers Fund, 1907
p. 194, p. 201	
p. 67	Pierpont Morgan Library
p. 70 (modern telescope)	Photograph from the Mount Wilson and Palomar Observatories
pp. 158–159, p. 216	John Murray, London, for *Mission From Cape Coast Castle to Ashantee,* by T. E. Bowdich (1819)
p. 213 (Blackfoot Indians)	Museum of the Plains Indian, Browning, Montana
p. 215	National Congress of American Indians, courtesy of Monarch Air Lines
p. 131	National Gallery of Canada, Ottawa
p. 105	National Museum, Copenhagen
p. 213 (Cheyenne Indians)	Northern Cheyenne Agency
pp. 276–277	Pan American World Airways
p. 22	Copyright reserved, South West Africa Expedition, Peabody Museum, Harvard University
p. 207	G. P. Putnam's Sons, for *Growth and Culture,* by Margaret Mead and Frances Macgregor (1951)

p. 52	H. Armstrong Roberts
p. 73	Copyright reserved, Royal Library, Windsor Castle
p. 211, p. 222, p. 302 (Eskimo)	Three Lions, Inc.
p. 124	University of Toronto, "Explorations Five," ed. by E. S. Carpenter (1955)
p. 262, p. 263, p. 272	Trans World Airlines, Inc.
p. 81 (Finn), p. 303 (2)	United Nations
p. 298	UNICEF
p. 308	U.S. Army Photograph
p. 282	The Viking Press, Inc., for *Lascaux Cave Paintings,* by Fernand Windels (1950)
p. 278–279	E. Weyhe, for *Ornament in Applied Art* (1924)
p. 83 (Chinese)	White Brothers from Monkmeyer
p. 217, p. 232, p. 291	Wide World Photos

ILLUSTRATION ACKNOWLEDGMENTS

The illustrations on pages 12, 16, 17, 29, 30–31, 33, 37, 40, 41, 42, 43, 49, 54, 55, 60, 62, 71, 77, 107, 114, 136, 144, 149, 151, 154, 157, 162, 169, 171, 172, 188, 190, 197, 199, 202, 203, 230, 235, 236, 237, 238, 239, 240, 242, 243, 245, 246–247, 251, 256, 257, 259, 268–269, 271, 272, 274, 275, 278–279, 294–295, and 296–297 are by Jan Fairservis. All others are by W. T. Mars.

Contents

MAN ASKS ABOUT MAN

MAN
LEARNS
ABOUT
MAN

Man's Discovery of Man

WHEREVER we find human beings, we find that they wonder about other people—the people who live across the mountain, in the next valley, or on the other side of the island. Even the simplest savages in the mountains of New Guinea or the jungles of South America know that there are other people who are different from themselves, who look different, walk differently, and speak a different language. If it is safe to get close to them, they may find that they smell different, too, because they eat different food and put different kinds of paint on their skin and hair. These little groups of people, who live in a very small known world, as early men, our remote ancestors, must once have lived, have names for the other peoples, while very often they simply call themselves "the people." But they have no idea how big the world is. Often they think of a large island as if it were the whole world with water all around it.

We can imagine what it was like at the very dawn of man's history, when man was still very small, much smaller than he is today. Then, at a distance, it would have been hard to tell the difference between a group of men and a group of large apes. Seeing another group at a distance, early men would stop and wonder: Are these creatures like ourselves, who can talk to each other, or are they those other creatures, somewhat like ourselves, who run on four legs almost all the time while we run on two legs almost all the time? Though such a little group of early men, who as yet had no clothes and were probably much hairier than modern man and who had only very simple weapons, might be as frightened of another little group of men as they were of a band of apes, they would be differently frightened. Because they would not yet have learned that the way they talked to each other was called a language and that the way these other men talked to each other was also a language, they would have felt that there was no way they could make friends.

You can work out what this would be like if a group of you—say some ten boys and girls—lived in one part of a wood or along a beach some ten miles long, and another group lived a whole day's walk away, and you both wandered about the woods or along the shore looking for animals to hunt or crabs to catch and for berries and nuts. If neither group had any permanent camping place, it might be weeks or even months before you met, and if you were frightened of each other, it would be easy for both of you to hide as long as you wanted to. You might become experts at finding signs of where the others had been—a leaf broken here, a branch pulled back there. If you already knew how to kindle a fire, you would find the ashes of the others' fires. Living like this, the only fights would be accidental ones that started because both groups got frightened when they suddenly met face to face. But if your group came to know the rocks and the streams and gave names to them and decided that one part of the woods or the beach belonged to you, then when members of the other group wandered into your territory you might get angry and try to scare them away or even attack them if they would not go. But actually, this would not happen to *you* in twentieth-century America, because your group could talk to the others and make friends with them, and together you could make rules about living next to each other.

This is what we think the early world must have been like, but all we know of it is what we can guess from the size and shape of the bones of early men, from the stone tools which they used and, later, from the pictures painted on the walls of caves and from the way the dead were buried. We have to fill in our picture by studying peoples who today still live in a very primitive way—peoples who know nothing about writing or metals or govern-

ments, and who know so little geography that they think that they themselves and the tribes over the next mountain are the only people there are in the world.

So we study the few savages who are left on this earth. But they themselves are fast becoming members of the modern world, for no one could go to study them if they were really completely isolated. From them we find out how little groups of people—sometimes forty or fifty, sometimes a few hundred—treat their neighbors, who speak another language and live a little differently. They have become partly friends, partly enemies. Sometimes they trade with each other, the fishermen who live on a river or at the seashore trading their fish for vegetables grown by the people who live away from the water. Some of the markets are carried on silently by the two groups, both carrying spears or bows and arrows, who meet at an appointed place and put the things they

have to exchange on middle ground. No words are spoken, for neither can speak the other's language. Both groups are wary; each is watching for the slightest hint that the other means to fight instead of trade. Sometimes when there is a fight between two groups, women and those children old enough to talk are carried off and learn to speak the language of their captors. Then a link may be formed between the two groups, for there are people who can translate from one language to the other. Cautious arrangements may be made for visits, and there may even be feasts. In time, groups of villages may become so friendly that it is very unusual for them to fight. They no longer think of one another as enemies or strangers and keep these words for the people over the *next* hill.

The world of primitive peoples like these may be very small, no more than twenty or thirty miles of mountain and forest.

Within it they may know every little stream and every rock, and they may have long stories to explain how each stream started, how each rock came to be there. But they do not yet know anything about making maps. And because they have no way of keeping records or of writing down what has happened, they can only think about the past in quite simple ways. Some people try to think about the past by memorizing the names of their fathers' and their fathers' fathers and their fathers' fathers' fathers, which is a little like memorizing the names of the presidents of the United States or of the kings and queens of England. Some people learn to make a winter count and make marks on a tree trunk or a special stick so they can count back and say, "It was five winters ago that we defeated the people on the other side of the hill," or "It was ten winters ago that a terrible storm broke down all the fruit trees we had planted."

A section of a calendar history (winter count) of the Kiowa. The vertical black poles indicate winters; the pictographs above and between them illustrate outstanding events of succeeding winters and summers.

All people have the sun and the moon to help them think about time. But thinking about time is easier for people who live in cold places, where winter is very different from summer, than it is for those who live in tropical places, where days and nights are all the same length. There they have had to count time by the changing direction of the winds or by the seasons when it rains or when the rivers rise. The moon helps them to mark off months, and this is easier still for people who live by the seaside, where they can watch the tides and learn to see how the high tides and the low tides come and go with the changes of the moon. From watching the sun and the moon, some peoples went on to watching constellations like the Dippers or stars like the Pleiades, and they could talk more accurately about the passing of time.

Of course, before people could say very much about how many winters before, or how many moons ago, something had happened, they had to be able to count. Counting probably began with people noticing clusters—three things or five things—and then beginning to match them in their minds with the five fingers on a hand and the five toes on a foot. Can you imagine how exciting it must have been when a people who had no words to count

anything with suddenly realized that they could use the same word for the number of fingers a human being has and for the number of toes? From this, it would take only one more step to divide up the five. But some people, instead of using the word *hand* for five, used other words, such as the word *dog* for four, and so moved from a dog to the idea of fourness. Some people put both hands together at once and counted by tens; other people put hands and feet together and counted by twenties.

Once people had a way of thinking about days, by calling them suns, and of thinking about nights, by calling them the time when there is no sun or the time when the stars shine, they could think about distance too. One man could ask another: "How far is it to the place where you found that strong stone out of which you have made that ax?"

And the other could answer: "I walked for five days toward the place where the sun rises, and I slept for five nights." In order to make this kind of answer, it was necessary already to have learned to watch the sun, to know where it rose and where it set, to think of days as the periods of time when the sun shines, and to count.

Then man could think about the little world he knew. One part was toward the rising of the sun, another toward the place where the sun set. When people did this accurately, they then had directions—east and west, north and south. Sometimes they included two more directions—the very top of the sky above (the zenith) and the very center of the earth beneath (the nadir). People who lived on islands sometimes thought, instead, of the center of the island as one direction and of the seashore as the other. This was a way of thinking about directions which was very useful on that island but no good at all when the people went to larger places.

Men lived in these very small known worlds, and there may have been many hundreds or thousands of them in many parts of the earth long before any bigger societies developed. Such little groups of men did not yet have any way of traveling very far. But sometimes part of a group would break away and wander, year after year, farther away from the place where they once had lived. So gradually a whole great island or even a continent could be inhabited by little groups of people who knew only a few neighbors and who had no way of knowing more of the world and no way of thinking about it. Even after they had invented small boats which made it possible to travel a little farther, to venture up and down long rivers or from island to island in the sea, when people settled down they knew only a few other peoples.

But they might remember. Sitting by the fireside, they might tell long tales about their wanderings and the heroes who had led them across the sea. Each people still believed that they lived in a little world, and each had their own idea about how it had begun. Some thought that the earth and the sky had once been close together but that children had been born in between and had pushed the earth and the sky apart. Others thought that the world rested on a turtle's back or that it was held in place by a great snake. Some thought that the world had been made specially, and that afterward the sun was placed in the sky and men and animals on the earth. Others treated the world as if it had always been there, but they had various ways of explaining how men came to live or how men came to die—for example, because they forgot how to shed their skin the way snakes do. In some explanations of how things came to be, all human beings—the people telling the story, their neighbors, and their enemies—were treated as if they were alike. But other people had stories to explain how they, "the people," had been created in a special way that made them different from anyone else.

Living in small groups that were isolated from one another, each people could work out a different idea about the beginning of the world, and there was no one to criticize their view. For people had not yet begun to look for evidence from which they could learn how men and animals developed on this earth and how the world itself began. And there were, of course, no great religions with holy books which told about the beginning of the world and man's place in the universe. Instead of arguing about the truth of different ideas, people listened to the ideas of other peoples as if they were stories and sometimes retold them, as stories, while they continued to believe that their own account was true—for themselves.

Each of these primitive peoples also worked out some idea of the future—where people go when they die, whether the world will last forever or whether it is in danger of being destroyed by a flood or by the sun's failing to rise, for example. Some peoples thought that at one time in the past the world had been a very good place, where it had always been summer or where there had been enormous amounts of good things to eat. Others thought that the good times were still to come in some future on earth or in the next world. Each people, or sometimes groups of people who had spread out over many miles of land or on many islands, had ideas about the world that satisfied them. But no methods had been invented to investigate any of these ideas. No one knew how to dig up the ground to find traces of earlier man or of animals that had disappeared, or how to count layers of different-colored rock that show how the climate has altered. From their imagining and wondering, people worked out explanations with which they were content. They worked out their ideas so slowly, generation after generation, that no one saw them as ideas made by men. Sometimes one people borrowed the ideas of another people because for some reason they seemed better than their own,

!Kung Bushmen, Kalahari Desert, South West Africa

but even in this case the ideas were already there. The earth and the sky, the sun and the moon, the stars and the planets, the tides and the seasons, the trade winds and the time of year when fish came up the river—these were always there, and the stories people told seemed always to have been there also.

Some of the peoples of the world have continued to live like this right down to the present day. In deep jungles, on high mountains, they still hunt and fish and fight and feast each other as men did early in human history. Usually these are peoples who wandered so far away that they never heard of the new inventions through which man became a creature who could build great cities, tunnel through mountains, sail the high seas, and finally fly through the air. And without these living primitive peoples it would be much harder for us to imagine what the life of our distant human ancestors was like.

But some early men did not stop with a life that depended upon hunting and fishing and gathering nuts and berries. They discovered that it was possible to plant seeds when and where one wanted to, so as to have a supply of food on which one could depend. This made an enormous difference. For then, instead of depending on the day's hunt and often going hungry or even starving to death, people could plan.

Because we have grown up in a world where food can be moved for thousands of miles, packed in cans and crates and bags, and where harvests are sometimes so good that people in one place have much more food than they need, it is hard for us to think about what it is like not to be able to keep food but to depend every day on what can be hunted or caught or picked. People who must do this try to remember where they found food last year. But sometimes, as in the deserts of Australia, there comes a bad year. A little group with nothing to eat will walk thirty miles to a water hole where they expect to find some bulbs that are fit to eat, and find none. Then they must leave the old and the weak behind them to die, because they can no longer walk and there is no way to carry them. Meanwhile the rest struggle on, getting weaker too, looking for another water hole or hoping to find an animal that has not died in the drought.

Two kinds of discoveries began to free mankind from this continual fear of starvation tomorrow—discoveries about preserving food and the discovery of agriculture. However, a people who discovered how to preserve fruits and nuts and the pith of palm trees before they had learned anything about planting seeds and making gardens might not make the next discovery, even if they had neighbors who had done so.

This is an important thing to remember about discoveries and inventions: Sometimes, instead of helping people to advance, a discovery or an invention holds them back. In New Guinea, people learned how to cut down sago palms, chopping up the soft

Sago working in New Guinea

pith to make a kind of meal that keeps for weeks. In this way they could stock up a supply of food for a feast, and whenever they needed more, there was always another tree to cut down. So they depend on sago and neglect their gardens.

Other peoples learned to preserve their catch of fish, and a few hours of fishing once a month or even a few days of fishing once a year gave them their major supply of food. This, too, could be so satisfactory a way of getting food that people were discouraged from the hard work of preparing the ground and cultivating food crops.

Fruit trees, which are planted only once and then give fruit regularly for many years, provide another way of getting a sure supply of food that is much easier than planting regular yearly gardens. The breadfruit trees of the South Pacific islands are an example, and the people there who cultivated the trees learned to preserve the breadfruit in great pits for years, against a time when a hurricane might devastate the island.

A different discovery about food came when men domesticated animals to use for eating and could then drive their future dinner around with them as flocks of sheep or herds of cattle, horses, or reindeer. When they learned also to use the hides of the cattle or the wool of the sheep, people established a kind of moving supply and could wander wherever their animals could find food for grazing while they themselves lived on the meat or milk and used the hides or wool to clothe and house themselves.

Other peoples learned to domesticate animals which would stay around the house—dogs, pigs, and chickens, and in the New World (so called because the Americas were new to our ancestors at the time of Columbus) turkeys, llamas, and guinea pigs. By combining the keeping of these animals with gardening, people had a reliable source of meat for special occasions and did not have to depend on hunting and fishing.

These various inventions were also combined by some peoples into true agriculture. When domesticated animals were harnessed to plows, men could begin to plant great fields of grain. And when they had learned complicated ways of controlling water, by using the rising of rivers or by distributing water in irrigation ditches, men could widely extend their good land. And the rice or wheat or barley which they grew could be stored from one year to the next.

Clothing as we find it today has several uses. It protects the

body from cold in cold climates and from heat in hot climates. It permits people to keep parts of their body covered except when they are alone or with members of the same sex or alone with their family. Clothing makes it possible to dress up, to show that it is a special day of the week or a birthday. It can be used as a uniform—to show the difference between a general and a private, a chief or prince and a commoner, to show who is the priest, or the elevator man, or the hostess on an airplane, or the policeman to whom you can go for help. It can be used to show the difference

between classes of people, between school children and adults, between the children who go to one school and those who go to another, between the players on two teams, between the rich and the poor. If you stop to think how many things it would be difficult to do if people wore no clothes, no ornaments, no rings, no earrings, no hats, and no arm bands at all—so that the only differences among them were sex and age and size—you can see how important an invention clothing was.

Human clothing is often compared to the feathers of birds or the antlers of deer or the bright colors of fish, and there are proverbs like "Fine feathers do not make fine birds." Human beings do use clothes as birds and animals use feathers or antlers or manes, that is, to tell others whether they are males or females, to make themselves attractive, and sometimes to show how strong and important they are and to keep younger and weaker creatures in their place. However, there is a real difference between the feathers of a bird and the colors of a butterfly's wings and the clothes worn by a human being. For the human being not only can take his clothes off, but also he can change their style altogether.

Changes in the colors of a butterfly's wings do happen, but they take many, many generations to develop. For instance, there is in England a species of moth which once had many speckled and only a few black members, but now these moths are mostly black, matching tree trunks that nowadays are coated with smoke. But if an army decides that the color of its uniform makes the men too easily seen, the uniforms can be changed overnight from blue to khaki. And human beings can borrow ideas about clothes from one another. They can buy the clothes and put them on immediately.

However, we have to think of early man as having no clothes at all, depending on hair to protect his head and more hair to protect his body. The earliest clothing was probably not what we would call clothing but rather jewelry or ornaments—bird feathers stuck in the hair, shells hung around the neck, arm bands made of straw into which bones and feathers could be fastened. Though people probably used their ears to keep ornaments in place before they learned to pierce them, we find all over the world the knowledge of making holes in the ear lobes for earrings. Some-

A variety of headdresses

times those holes are enormous, weighted down with very heavy rings or filled with ornaments at one time of life and left empty at another. In New Guinea you can still find people who wear great headdresses of bird-of-paradise feathers but no other clothes at all. Even there, however, people are modest, though being "dressed" only means wearing one earring. A well-behaved girl would not go out in public without one.

We do not know what the first clothes were made of, because unlike ornaments of shell and bone, clothes rot away and leave no trace. From the evidence of existing peoples, we know about clothes made from the bark of trees, which is beaten until it is soft or pliable or pasted in layers to make it strong. We also know about clothes made by shredding leaves into narrow strips, and we know about clothes made of animal skins. Then there are the various beginnings of weaving—nets into which feathers are fastened, matting made of narrow strips of leaves. Then, when

Ways of traveling by water

Ways of traveling by land

fibers could be spun into thread, true cloth could be woven. Each of these inventions took many steps, and most of the discoveries man made about how to tan hides, plait leaves, spin threads, and set up looms for weaving cloth are still used today. Our shoes are made from hides tanned in great vats which prepare hides for thousands of shoes at once. The cloth for our clothes is woven in strips measured in thousands of feet instead of in inches. But the ways of doing these things were invented thousands of years ago as people struggled to cover their bodies from the cold and to protect themselves as they slept.

Another set of inventions had to do with moving things, especially food, from one place to another. Here we have two lines of discovery: ways of traveling by water and ways of traveling on land. Travel by water depended on the invention of something that would stay afloat, such as a raft or a bull boat (a kind of tub made of hides or rushes) or a dugout canoe or a skin boat. They had to be able to carry human beings and their possessions, and be moved along in some way, as with a punting pole, a paddle, or an oar. Then it was necessary to find ways of giving a boat power, either by having a whole team of rowers or paddlers or else by using a sail which caught the wind. Once one of these two methods had been developed, it was possible to transport food and materials for long distances wherever there were waterways.

Traveling overland, it was possible to move only small loads as long as human beings were the only carriers, especially if they had to carry their food with them as well. Carrying poles, which make it possible for more than one man to move something—a sick person or a large game animal—were some improvement over one man's carrying a load by himself, but the amount of energy used by each man was the same. Heavier things could be carried, but not more things. Only when animals had been domesticated and man could use a donkey or a camel or a dog or a llama did overland travel with food become possible. The real advances, however, came with the invention of the sledge, or travois, by means of which men or animals could pull even very heavy things over the ground, the sled for travel over snow, and—much later—the wheel. Basically, carts are platforms or boxes on wheels in which, because they are easily moved, large numbers of things can be transported without the use of more energy than was needed when men or animals carried small loads on their backs. Today we are still making this shift from what one human being can carry to what can be carried on wheels, as in the little folding shopping carts that people take to grocery stores and the carts that are being put in airports so that old ladies can push their own heavy luggage around.

Once people had learned to plan their food supply and had both the means of transporting it and of storing it, it was possible for more people to live close together in cities. Other things, such as fuel and clothes, or the materials for clothes and tools and weapons, had to be transported too. Then the size of a city depended on how much water and food and how many other materials could be brought to it in reliable ways. Archaeologists believe that some ancient cities fell because these things became too difficult to do.

As more people lived together, it was necessary to invent ways of regulating their lives so that they would not murder each other or steal from each other and so that they could act together to provide for themselves. Living together in large numbers called for a great many new inventions. Some form of government was necessary, and laws were needed to control the behavior of people who were strangers to each other. Work had to be divided up. Some people grew food, some gathered fuel, some made materials for clothing or tools or weapons, and some moved things from one place to another. Markets were needed, where people could buy from one another, and there had to be some kind of money to use for exchange.

All these inventions had been made by peoples living in smaller groups, even when they were less necessary. In the South Seas we find people who used dog's teeth for money, tiny tribes whose chiefs ruled as kings, villages that specialized—one in

A variety of objects used as money

growing vegetables and another in fishing. But when, instead of living in little tribes and little villages, people began to live in great cities, all these separate inventions had to be brought together.

In these large societies we find writing, too, as a next great step in human history. And as soon as people could write, they did not have to depend on the memory of living people or the stories that old people told, but could keep the knowledge of a past beyond the memory of anyone alive. As they could keep records, they could begin to know what was happening to them and to ask new questions: Was the kingdom getting larger or smaller? Did the river rise at the exact same time every year? And because all the special knowledge—how to govern, how to pray, how to make offerings to the gods, how to plant crops, or how to temper metal—no longer had to be carried in their heads, it could even be lost and learned again as long as people could read what had been written down. Civilization as we think of

Excavations at Deir el Bahri, Egypt, 1929–31

it seems to have started approximately five thousand years ago.

Nowadays, in order to get a picture of what these early civilizations were like, we have to depend almost entirely on the results of digging up buried cities. In the New World at the time the Spaniards arrived, there were two great flourishing centers of civilization—the Aztecs of Mexico and the Incas of the highlands of Peru. About these peoples we have partial descriptions written by their conquerors. The Aztecs had a kind of picture-writing, but the Incas had no writing at all. However, the Incas had invented a way of recording numbers and of sending messages to distant parts of the empire by the use of complicated knotted cords, called *quipus,* by means of which a messenger could jog his memory. In Yucatan, the more ancient Maya—from whom the Aztecs had got the idea for their writing—had discovered the idea of zero (which the Greeks and Romans had not succeeded in doing), and using the mathematics and astronomy they devel-

oped, had invented a calendar so complicated that they could think about cycles of 144,000 days. But for older civilizations which disappeared long ago from both the New World and the Old, we have to depend entirely on the work of archaeologists.

By careful work—by comparing one building dug up here with another one dug up there, by matching the kinds of paintings found on the walls and the pieces of clay pots found in both buildings, by comparing the things made in a city with those brought there from some other place—archaeologists can build up a partial picture of how the people of these great kingdoms lived. So we know that for the peoples who lived in cities the picture of the world had changed. Instead of an area of ten or twenty square miles, they now knew about areas of hundreds of miles, within which taxes were collected and soldiers were recruited and across which riches were brought to ornament palaces and temples. And within the same kingdom there were great contrasts in the ways of living at the center and farther away, in the city and in the country. For a people living in a little tribe, the important differences are those between themselves and the people of the next tribe, who live in the next valley, speak a different language, and have different customs. But now, for people living in cities and kingdoms, differences inside the society became important. There were rulers and priests and common people and, often, slaves; people whose work was honored and people whose work was despised. Only a few people knew how to read and write, so there was a great difference between the people who *knew* and the people who did not, as well as between those who were rich and noble and those who were poor or of humble birth. With writing, people could keep long records of the past and many kinds of records about the present; with boats and chariots they could travel great distances. When one of these kingdoms conquered another or when a kingdom fell apart—for lack of materials to build palaces or lack of slaves to do the work, or because of long, bloody fights over who was to be the next ruler—the inventions they had made would be kept and used by the next kingdom that rose to take the place of the one that had fallen.

So the peoples of Babylon and Egypt, ancient China, Greece, and Rome learned from one another. The knowledge of stars and planets accumulated. It was possible to make more complicated calendars. And men could begin to wonder how the stars, the sun, and the earth came to be and what held them in the sky. Mathematics and geometry developed as it became necessary to keep records of huge taxes and to calculate the dimensions of great buildings like the pyramids in Egypt or the Parthenon at Athens. People could measure more, and could do so more accurately; they could keep longer and more complicated records; they could travel longer distances and move more rapidly; they could think about a longer future.

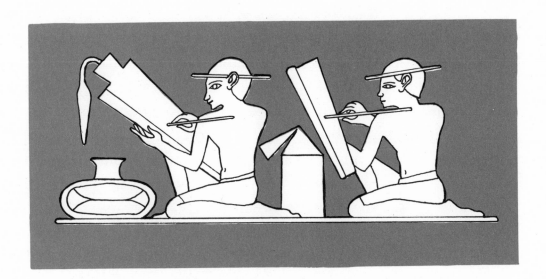

Man As a Being

JUST as from earliest times man has wondered and built theories about the world around him and the sky above his head and the people of other tribes, so also man has wondered about himself as a living creature living in a world of living creatures. As man hunted and trapped and fished, he learned a great deal about the ways of animals and birds and fish, and he had the kind of brain that made it possible for him to be curious and to classify things.

This is just what we do when we play the game "Animal, vegetable, mineral." First we place the thing which the person who is IT has to guess in a big class of "Things that are alive and can move" (animal), or "Things that are alive and cannot move" (vegetable), or "Things that are not alive" (mineral). This is a pretty clumsy set of classifications, but it is a beginning. If the

38

correct answer is "Animal" (standing loosely for all living creatures), then the next question can be, "Is it a bird or a fish?" If the answer is "No," then if you know some biology, you can ask, "Is it a mammal?" That is, is it the kind of creature that does not lay eggs but protects the body of the infant inside the mother until it is strong enough to be born? If the answer is "Yes," you can start to divide up the mammals into the kinds of creatures that live in herds and eat grass (such as cows and sheep and goats), or the kinds of creatures that eat other animals (this includes lions and tigers and men), or the kinds of creatures that have hands (this includes apes, monkeys, and men), and so on. It is as if the world were made up of boxes and boxes within boxes, each with many kinds of things in it, and by asking such questions, you can divide up the whole world in which the object you are trying to guess is placed, until you find the box which contains the answer. If you are to find a human being, the answer will be, "It is a living creature—a mammal that eats meat, has hands, walks erect, and uses language and tools."

Just as we do, early men and primitive men also noticed the living world around them and arranged it in their minds into sets of boxes—containing things they thought were related to each other. Some people put men into one box and women and children—boys and girls both—into another box as if the difference between them was almost as great as, for example, the difference between a man and a monkey. Some put all the people of their own tribe into one box, but treated the people of other tribes as if they were more like animals than like themselves. When they met another people whose skin was of a different color, or whose hair was straighter or curlier than their own, or who had a differently shaped nose, they had to decide whether to put them in a box with themselves, as human beings, or to treat them as another kind of creature.

But there were also many other ways in which people could think about human beings and other living things. Was a man more like a bird, which has two legs, than like a dog, which has four? Was a man in some way related to a fish or a frog because he could swim in the water as well as walk on the land? Did color matter? If a man had black skin, did this make him closer to a black bear than to a white bear, and was a white man more

like a white bear or a white parrot than he was like a man with
a black skin? Other peoples, looking at the differences between
individuals, divided them up into sky people and earth people, or
into sun people and moon people. Everywhere we find that
people struggled to find out what made living things different
from rocks, wondering whether a moving stream was alive or
not, wondering about man himself.

When they decided that trees, or rivers, or the sea, or the sun and moon were somehow alive because they moved, they sometimes thought of them as inhabited by spirits or gods and goddesses. Some peoples thought of trees as inhabited by spirits whom one had to treat very politely if one wanted to cut the tree down. Similarly, some peoples decided that all birds and all animals were different from all men, but others thought that only some birds and some animals were different. So, if a man who was out hunting found a special bird that looked at him in a more intelligent way than most birds did, he might think of that bird as an ancestor or a spirit that once had been a human being or someday would be one again. Even today, knowing how much our own dog or cat knows and feels about us, we feel that it is somehow more human and less like dogs and cats in general. The whole question of just where human beings belong in the living world, where they have come from, what makes them act as they do, puzzled—and still puzzles—people who live in small groups and have to work out answers for themselves without the help of what other people have thought.

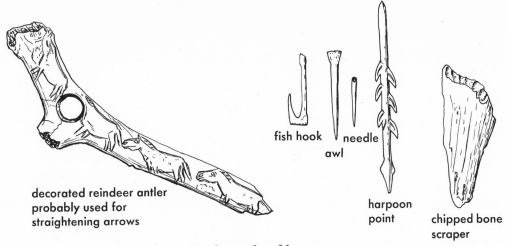

decorated reindeer antler
probably used for
straightening arrows

fish hook needle
awl

harpoon
point

chipped bone
scraper

Tools made of bone

All the peoples we know anything about recognize that living things have a beginning and an end, that they are in some way born and that they die. Also, men must have found out very early that wounds are dangerous and if blood flows too long and too freely from a cut, somehow life seems to flow away too, and the fish or bird or animal or man dies. So all sorts of ideas grew up about blood, and rules were made about shedding another man's blood, which was another way of talking about killing him. Rules were even made about what people could do with their own blood—for instance, if they wanted to prick patterns on their skin as in tattooing. Sometimes only a special relative, such as a mother's brother, could shed a boy's blood. For people knew enough about how children are born to know that a mother and baby "share" the same blood, and they might go on to think of a person's blood as something that belonged to his mother's family.

Because they caught fish and hunted birds and animals and could compare the leg bone of a wild animal with the leg bone of a man who had hurt himself in such a way that the bone stuck out, people also knew about bones very early. They knew a good deal about how strong bones are, because they used bones to make heads of spears and arrows, fish hooks, and harpoon points;

and they sometimes carved them into toys or little statues. Just as blood came to be thought of as something very precious, representing life, and as something one shared with one's relatives—an idea we still find in our language today when we speak about "blood relatives" as compared to relatives-in-law—so in the same way bones came to represent strength and sometimes courage. In daring someone to do an act of bravery, one man might say to another, or a woman might say to a man, "If you have bones, you will do this thing." And we say of a weak man, "He hasn't any backbone."

Everywhere in the world, peoples learned that loss of blood endangers life, and they also learned something about how a human skeleton is put together. But how good their ideas were about human skeletons depended a little on the kinds of animals they hunted. For even though they came upon the bones of people long dead, the bones might have fallen apart, and no one could be quite sure how the bones had once fitted together.

There were a great many other things which we take for granted today but about which early man or primitive men knew nothing. They did not know, for example, how the heart pumps the blood through the body; nor did they have any idea of how the blood leaves the heart, flows through the body, and comes back again. The very word "vessel," which we use today for arteries and veins, reminds us of a time when men knew nothing about the circulation of the blood, when they thought of veins and arteries simply as containers. Some peoples did know that a way of telling whether a person was dead or alive was by listening for the heartbeat, and some knew that one could tell that a person was alive by his breathing. But because they did not understand anything about how the heart and the lungs worked, they were often confused and uncertain.

Sleep was puzzling, too. People could see that being asleep is somewhat like being dead. A sleeping person lies very still and does not answer when he is spoken to, but when he wakes up he is just as alive as ever. So some peoples built up theories about sleep and believed that when a man is asleep his soul goes off on a journey, and explained his dreams as the wonderful adventures his soul has while his body sleeps. Dreams are things that happen inside a person. But puzzling things happened outside too. When a man knelt by a clear pool, who was the other man looking up at him from the pool, who smiled when he smiled and frowned when he frowned?

And shadows were puzzling. Could one harm a man by sticking a magic spear through his shadow? And could one explain the difference between a human being and a spirit or a ghost by saying that a man cast a shadow but a spirit or a ghost did not? Some peoples thought that the shadow represented man's soul, and seeing the double shadow cast at noonday, they sometimes thought of man as having two souls.

As people wondered about the difference between being alive and dead, awake and asleep, they also wondered about being sick. One day a person was strong and well—a man could walk many miles over the mountains tracking a tiger or a bear, or a woman could carry a heavy load on her back or fish all day on the reef. But the next day this strong person did not feel like moving; perhaps his arm or leg hurt, or he did not want to eat, or if he did eat something, he could not keep it in his stomach. What did this mean? Did it mean he was going to die? People worked out different ideas about what made a person get sick. Maybe he had done something wrong, or an angry person had bewitched him, or he had accidentally broken off the branch of a tree belonging to a god. Without any knowledge of how the human body works, they had to try to build theories of what made men sick and what would make them well again. Was it necessary to find the sorcerer and pay him, or to make an offering to the angry god, or to confess to a secret sin, or to pay off a neglected debt? For primitive peoples, sickness was an important problem and a reason for thinking about human beings, just as today we know how important it is to find cures and ways of preventing sickness and men are willing to study for years to become doctors and we build great hospitals for taking care of the sick and have health departments to keep our food, water, and air pure.

Then there was the question of food. Every known people recognizes that there is a relationship between eating food and feeling strong, between not eating food and feeling hungry and weak. They know, too, that food is necessary for life, even though some peoples think that a man should be proud of being able to go hungry, so hungry that he can press the front of his stomach against his backbone to show that there is "nothing" in between. Many peoples felt that although food was necessary for everyday life, when one was going to do something very important—run a race, go on a difficult hunting trip, perform a religious ceremony —it was necessary to go without food, to fast. And feasts were a way of celebrating a successful hunt, a victory, a birth or a marriage, or the end of mourning.

Peoples everywhere have set times for eating, though they may eat only one meal a day and snacks in between, or may never eat breakfast. If work was to be done—if men were to go hunting or into the forest for wood to build a house or a canoe, if women were to work in their gardens—it was convenient for people to be hungry at particular times. For if everyone expected to eat at a particular time of day, women could get the food ready, men could come home, and children could come in from play. On dark, cloudy days, when it was impossible to see where the sun was in the sky or where the shadows lay, there was no way of telling what time it was except by how hungry one was. But once men had learned to eat regularly, their stomachs became a kind of clock to help them measure time *inside,* while they were learning to watch the sun and the moon and to listen to the cries of birds in the night to measure time *outside.*

However, knowing that if one does not eat, one gets hungry and that if one does not eat for a long time, one will die of starvation does not mean that people understood what food does for the body. They could see that birds ate and animals ate, that some young animals had to be fed milk, and that human babies needed their mothers' milk from the time they were born. They could also realize that it is necessary to drink water, that without water one's throat gets dry and one becomes thirsty. People who had been lost on a desert or in a canoe at sea sometimes returned to tell terrible stories of the way it felt to have no water to drink. Just as in many different ways blood and bones inside the body stood for life and strength, so, too, food and water stood for strength and life outside the body. Many ways were thought of to use the life-giving quality of water. It was brought from a special sacred spring or was blessed in a religious ceremony and made holy so that it would bless those who drank it, or bathed in it, or over whose heads and hands it was poured.

People learned not to eat poisonous things and to keep waste products and dead things away from drinking water so that it would be safe for people to drink. Though they did not understand what it was about body wastes and dead things that made water impure, they knew it was so. Sometimes this meant that they moved their camps a little distance every day; sometimes it meant that water had to be carried from far away because people buried their dead close to the houses inside a village.

Later, when men came to live in cities and forgot many of the things they had known in the forest, they stopped being careful about water. They used the same rivers or canals to bathe, to dump wastes and dead things into, to wash their dishes and clothes, and to get water for drinking. This is an example of how the first forward steps in civilizations may sometimes also look like steps backward. When men stopped living in little groups out in the forests or in the fields and plains, and gathered together in great cities, life was less carefully protected until very recently when we began to learn something about germs and how disease is carried.

Some peoples did not have any idea that food, or a part of it, stays in the body. They thought that food simply was taken in and then passed out again. When human beings felt hungry they filled their stomachs, as you might give a baby a ball to hold when he reaches out his hand for something. But even when they recognized that something in food must stay in the body to help it grow and be strong, they still built up many strange theories. For instance, people believed that eating large round fruits gave one boils or warts, that hot peppery foods would make one willing to fight, that eating the flesh of a swift-footed animal would make one swift-footed also. Because people did not know what it is about the food or in the food that does make an animal or a human being grow, they worked out theories. And most of the theories were wrong, except those about which foods were poisonous or had definite medical properties, for then they could see what happened to those who ate them.

As men wondered what keeps people alive and well, they also wondered about birth. They knew quite well, of course, that human babies, like many other young animals—kittens and puppies, lambs and tiger cubs—are carried inside their mothers' bodies until they are sufficiently well developed to live outside. They also knew that birds and crocodiles and snakes lay eggs and that the young are protected not inside the mother's body but inside the

Embryonic development of a chick

egg. Often they would find eggs, and having no way of knowing whether they were freshly laid or whether there were little birds in them almost ready to hatch, they would break them open. In this way they learned quite a lot about the changes that go on inside an egg—from something liquid, just white and a yolk, to something more and more like a bird. Some peoples applied what they learned about birds to animals and human beings, and they thought these, too, must have eggs inside of them out of which the young are hatched. Other peoples were more impressed by watching a tiny bird grow into a big bird or a tiny animal grow into a big animal, and they thought that human beings must start out as creatures exactly like full-grown persons but very, very tiny.

Many peoples wondered where the little human being had been before he was born. They did not think of him as having a new beginning with a father and a mother, but instead thought that a father and a mother simply made a place for him to come into the world. Some peoples thought that a new baby was a grandfather or great-grandfather come back again into the world, and so they came to think of living in this world and another world as being rather like having two homes, a winter home and a summer home, for instance. Part of the time a man or a woman would be living on earth—being born as a baby, growing up through childhood and adolescence to adulthood, marrying, having children, and then dying, that is, going back to the other home from which they would later return to earth. Other peoples thought that the place from which infants came was different from the place to which one went when one died. And some peoples did think of each human being as something new and without any previous existence before the mating of his parents.

What different peoples did about names expressed their ideas about newborn children. Sometimes a child had to be named after an ancestor or else after someone recently dead and was then believed to have the soul of the person after whom he was named. Then it might be forbidden for two living persons ever to have the same name, and so also for a child to be named after a living person. We ourselves have various rules about names. If a boy is given the same first name as his father, we put "junior" after it to show that he is not the same person but the son of the man with the same name. But if a boy is named after his uncle, we call him not "junior" but "second" to show that he is not the son of the man but the second member of the family to have the same name. So even among ourselves, the relationship between who one is and what one's name is and the question of whether other people, inside and outside the family, have the same name are still important. One's last name is a way of saying who one's biological or adopted parents are, of establishing who one's family is. A name is part of yourself. It is often confusing if other people have the same name, and you care how people treat your name.

Primitive peoples had various ideas about the connection between the child and his mother and his father. Besides recognizing that the infant and the mother shared the same blood, some peoples worried about the food a woman ate while she was pregnant. Therefore she might be forbidden to eat frogs because they would make the baby jump about; or she might not be allowed to eat red fruit because the baby's skin would be marked. They knew just enough to realize that the food the mother eats is important for the growth and health of the baby, but they did not understand how it works. So they made many different kinds of rules about what a pregnant woman could or could not eat, and sometimes they made rules about what the father could eat, because they did not know just where the connection between a father and his child's looks and health begins and ends.

Primitive peoples could see that children look like their relations—sometimes like a mother, sometimes like a father, and

sometimes like a grandparent who was dead but was remembered. When they explained the likeness between a child and his mother by the idea that they shared the same blood, they had to have another way of explaining why a child resembled his father. So they might think that his soul came from his father or that, somehow, the spirits of the father's family shaped him or gave him his bones.

Many thousands of years of wondering and watching went into trying to understand birth, and only in the last fifty years have we come to understand to some extent how inheritance works and how a child can inherit traits like the color of his eyes or hair from either parent.

How people think was another puzzling question. From the time we can talk and understand what is said around us, modern children learn that thinking goes on inside the head in something called the brain, although it may be many years before children get a good idea of what a brain looks like. Primitive children had many more chances to see what physical brains look like, both those of animals and those of human beings, but many peoples made no connection between brains and thinking. For example, they might locate memory in the stomach. So if a boy was going to be taught a long charm to help make his garden grow, which he would have to memorize word for word because there was no writing, he would fast in order to be sure his stomach was empty; he might even take something to make him throw up to be absolutely sure it was empty. Then the words he learned could be safely put away, or so he thought, at the bottom of his stomach. And afterward he would eat a big meal to pack the words down tightly so he would never forget them. Another people thought that all thinking went on in the throat, where it is possible to feel the words one is saying, and they called changing a man's mind "twisting his neck."

Each people, before men began to observe very carefully the relationship between head injuries and difficulties in thinking, worked out a theory of their own to explain thought and to talk about it. They did this also with the common human feelings such as love and grief and fear and anger. Some peoples thought grief was something that happened to their eyes, because most people weep when they are sad. And fear was placed in various parts of the body—in the big toe which goes ahead of one into the grass and is the first part to touch a snake; or in the buttocks; or, as our language still reminds us, in the pit of the stomach; or in the spine where one can get a "chilly feeling." But the stomach could be thought of as the place where anger lived, instead of memory or fear. A people's theories about where in their bodies their feelings were located had an effect on how they actually felt. A people who, like ourselves, think of blushing with shame as something that happens in one's face do turn red when they are embarrassed. But a people who locate shame in the edges of the shoulders feel blood rush there when they are embarrassed. All these ideas were the result of human beings notic-

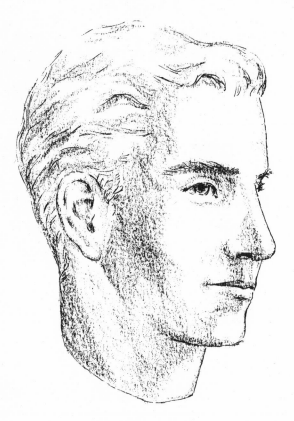

European Caucasoid

American Mongoloid
(Indian)

ing how they felt—how their eyes smarted from the salt of tears, how their stomach fluttered or their skin turned cold and clammy when they were scared, how their stomach ached when they were angry. Because they did not know what really controls human feeling, they did the best they could by making into a theory what some people said they felt. And because the people reporting on their eyes or their stomach or their fingers and toes were all members of the same human race, quite often some of these ideas are very much alike.

Another problem human beings thought about as they thought

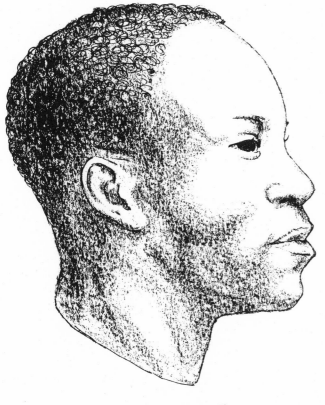

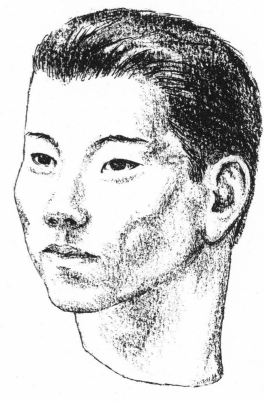

African Negroid

Asiatic Mongoloid

about themselves was the question of why some individuals are so much bigger or smaller, handsomer or uglier, brighter or more stupid than others. Such differences as these exist among every people we know about; even among the children in one family there are great differences. In an attempt to explain something they did not understand, some peoples seized on the idea of setting apart one man, and later his children, or a whole family or a group of families to be rulers who were then treated as if they were all nobler or more intelligent than others. Often this seemed to work. For if from early childhood a group of people are treated as if they are different from others, they do turn out that way: they walk more proudly, hold their heads higher, are surer that they are right. But then, when in such familes children were born who were not tall and beautiful and clever, as is always likely to happen, people who had accepted the idea that noble children come from noble families had to explain how this came about.

These natural differences among individual human beings have been explained in many ways. Sometimes the stars were made responsible, and we ourselves still say, "He was born under a lucky star." Or people decided that it was the day, or even the hour, of one's birth that mattered not only for what one was but also for what one could do. Then, before two people could marry, their horoscopes would be cast by a holy man to find out whether or not they were well matched.

Just as people had a great deal of trouble understanding differences between individuals—between brothers and sisters, between cousins, and between members of the same village—the differences between groups of people were also troublesome. It was only too easy to think that groups who did not look like each other

—because some were tall and some were short, some were black-skinned and some white-skinned, some had heavy eyelids which made their eyes look slanting and some did not, some had tight, thin lips and some had full, thick lips—really were unlike each other in other ways.

Sometimes people put ideas together in clusters. For example, night was a very frightening time to early man, for he had no candles and no lamps, no lights except his campfire and possibly a torch made of dry wood or leaves. If the fire went out, it took a long time to make a new one by rubbing together bits of wood or bamboo. When there was no moon, the forest was dark

and forbidding. Anything could happen. This is, of course, the way small children still may feel when their mother turns out the light and goes away. So anything that suggested night was also frightening, and because things that are frightening are thought of as bad things, the night, the dark, blackness, and monsters were thought of together. When this happened, people were afraid of other people with darker skins and regarded them as evil or dangerous. The opposite thing could also happen. White is the color of bones, and all over the world bones are put together with ideas about dead persons and about ghosts. When the first white men landed in Australia, the black-skinned people of Australia thought they must be ancestors come back from the dead. So white and light can be frightening, too.

When men met other men different from themselves—men who looked different, spoke a different language, lived in different kinds of houses, used different tools and weapons, married their wives and buried their dead in different ways—this was something they had to try to understand. The first step was to make sure that they were beings like themselves, not animals or spirits. But this was only a first step.

It was still possible to believe that men inherit ways of behaving from their ancestors. Just as they are human beings with human hearts and brains because their ancestors were human, it followed that they like certain foods, believe in their gods, and are trustworthy or treacherous, warlike or peace-loving, because of their ancestors. So it was possible to believe that a man was a brave, cruel, copper-skinned Indian because his parents were brave, cruel, copper-skinned Indians, or that a man was a cheerful, skillful, squat, twinkle-eyed Eskimo because his parents were cheerful, skillful, squat, twinkle-eyed Eskimo. It was easy to believe this because not only do children look like their parents, but usually they also speak the same language, eat the same kind of food, and behave in the same way. Even today, when people speak of Frenchmen as "Frogeaters," they are not always sure whether they mean that people who are brought up in France learn to like to eat frogs or that somehow French children are born with a liking for frogs. The same problem sometimes puzzles people when they think about languages. When Americans who have struggled long and hard to learn even a little French, go to France for the first time, it may be a surprising discovery that even French *children* speak French perfectly!

Only very slowly have we learned what human beings inherit from their ancestors and what they learn from their parents and how much little babies learn in the first months of their lives, so that by the time they can talk they seem to have been born knowing how to make French sounds—or English sounds or Chinese sounds.

So man has struggled to understand what a human being is: what it means to be alive instead of being something like a rock; what it means to be alive and move instead of being rooted to one place like a plant; what it means to be alive and move like an animal and know that one is alive and can move—in fact, to know one is a human being.

These are questions it has taken man perhaps a million years to try to answer: to find out the meaning of birth and how an individual is related to his ancestors and the past, and the meaning of death and how an individual is related to the next generation and the future; to find out how the human body works, how thinking goes on, and what happens when we feel sorrow or fear or anger or joy; to find out the meaning of differences between brothers and sisters and between peoples of the races which come from Europe and Africa and Asia.

With each increase in knowledge of this kind human beings become more the masters of their way of life and less helplessly

dependent on theories which had to be made up without knowledge. But even more important than the knowledge itself is
man's desire for knowledge, his endless curiosity about how he
came to be, what he is doing on earth, and what his fate will be
after death. And this hunger and thirst for knowledge civilized
children and men of today and primitive children and men share
with one another.

The Anthropologist at Work

ALL through history man has wondered about many things and has tried to find satisfactory ways of explaining them. Wonder is very important, because if we never wondered, we would never get to the point of asking questions. Yet wonder may lead people to write poetry or to paint pictures or to pray, as well as to ask the kinds of questions about the world and themselves that can be answered by science. Science means asking a question and keeping that question in one's head while one watches, over and over again, what happens until one finds an explanation. It means testing out the explanation—watching and watching again to see if the explanation works.

Early man had to do something like this in order to learn how to plant seeds. Someone who had watched seeds falling to the ground and then had seen the sprouts appear had to get the idea, "These are going to be plants." This looks simple to us, but it took early men hundreds of thousands, perhaps more than a million, years to realize this and then to get the next idea, "If plants grow from seeds, then I can put the seeds of the plants I want in the ground, and later I can eat the plants or their fruits." Hundreds of generations of men must have wandered through forests and over plains, hunting and fishing and returning each year at the same time to the same places to eat berries and fruits without recognizing how the plants grew or that they themselves could make a garden.

Very early in man's history the same kind of thing happened with tools. Even the earliest men must have used sticks for digging and stones which they picked up for hammering and chop-

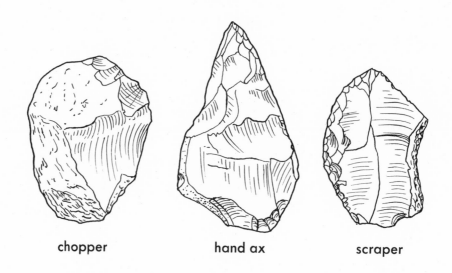

chopper   hand ax   scraper

ping and cutting. But the earliest tools that have been preserved and that we can recognize as having been made on purpose are large water-smoothed pebbles that were split in half by man; sometimes the sharp edge was chipped to make it sharper. Then, about half a million years ago, early men began to make better tools out of flint or quartzite or other brittle kinds of stone. Flint is both very hard and very brittle; when it is dropped hard or hammered, it splits into pieces with very sharp edges. Flint comes in oval lumps, called nodules, which are covered with a softer crust, but early men must have picked up and used unshaped, broken pieces of flint and may have repaired the sharp edge by chipping it when it got dull or nicked. Then in different parts of the world, early men began to make various sorts of tools by knocking big flakes off a nodule of flint and using these, or else by knocking off flakes to turn the core of the nodule itself into a tool. Some of these tools made of cores English-speaking archaeologists have named "choppers"; others they have named "hand axes." The hand ax—a tool shaped something like a huge almond, round at one end and pointed at the other with two shaped sides—has been found in a great many places. Men continued to make hand axes, improving but not changing them, for about a quarter of a million years. The same men used the flakes chipped off nodules to make different sorts of cutting and scraping and boring tools.

We have seen that human beings have been curious about themselves and the world around them—about the sun and the moon and the stars, about the tides and the fish that come to spawn, about how plants grow, how birds build their nests and hatch their eggs, how young animals are born. Because they were curious and watched what happened where seeds fell or when birds pecked their way out of eggs, human beings learned a great deal about the world. But none of this was science.

Science involves several things. It involves asking questions about the natural world, the universe: how it came to be, how it works, what it is, and what man's place in it is. Although most primitive peoples about whom we know have asked some of these questions, they have not done so systematically, moving from one question to the next, building up a theory about the nature of the world. The Greeks are the first people of whom we have any record who began to ask questions of this kind in a systematic way.

Aztec calendar stone
(Reproduction, Hayden Planetarium, New York)

Science also involves making observations, looking very carefully at the same thing over and over again. But observation is not the same thing as experimenting, and the recognition that it is possible to experiment as well as to watch is still another step necessary to the building of science.

At its simplest, to experiment means to try something out to see if or how it works. Many of the things that early man and primitive man discovered must have been learned through a combination of observation and experiment. Some primitive peoples have very complicated dyes, for instance, a beautiful red which is made by combining the green sap of a plant with a green berry. Someone must have seen this happen, by accident, and then must have experimented until he made it happen again. Once this experimental state of mind develops, a people are able to use their ability to watch what is going on in the world and can learn to do more and more things. In the South Seas a threadlike rainbow-colored creature, which looks like bright-colored spaghetti, comes up to the surface of the ocean once a year in October and November. The Samoans have learned when this happens, and they are there in their canoes with torches and nets, ready to make a haul. They know that if there is only a small haul in the third quarter of the moon in October, then the big haul will come in the third quarter of the moon in November.

But there is a long step between simply making an observation and trying out to see if it is correct—by keeping track of time and then going out to see if the fish are there again—and planning an experiment as scientists do, to find out more about a new metal, or to test a theory, or to search for a new substance.

For observation and experiment and checking to see if what one thinks is true continues to be true under the same and under different conditions, great accuracy is necessary. This means that there must be some way of recording what has been observed and tried out. We think that the first scientific work of this kind came about through long watching of the moon and the stars and the planets. When, through observations of the stars, men had worked out the length of a year—from which they could predict, for instance, the yearly rising of a river—and when they had learned to distinguish between planets and fixed stars and could predict eclipses of the moon, we have the beginnings of astronomy. In the civilizations of Egypt (in the Nile Valley) and Mesopotamia (in the valley of the Tigris ánd Euphrates rivers in the Middle East) town life began around 4000 B.C. In both of these civilizations a system of writing was developed very early, and a great deal of knowledge based on observations of the heavens was acquired and recorded. The Mesopotamians kept records of their star watching for hundreds of years, and it was indirectly from them that the Greeks and still later Western Europeans learned most of the astronomy known before 1600 A.D. But in Egypt and Mesopotamia these careful observations were not joined with imaginative thinking about the nature of man in the universe. Rather, what was known was used either for practical purposes, such as setting dates for planting crops or for holding ceremonies, or for casting horoscopes, for deciding when a journey should be started or whether a battle should be joined.

Still another idea was needed before a scientific study of the universe could be developed. This was the idea that man himself, as a conscious and separate being, could study the world around him, make observations and experiments, and build theories out of the results of what he learned. Again it was the Greeks who first really developed this idea, when they began to think not only about the universe but also about the process of thinking itself.

However, the modern approach to the world that combined conscious thinking and conscious experiment really developed in

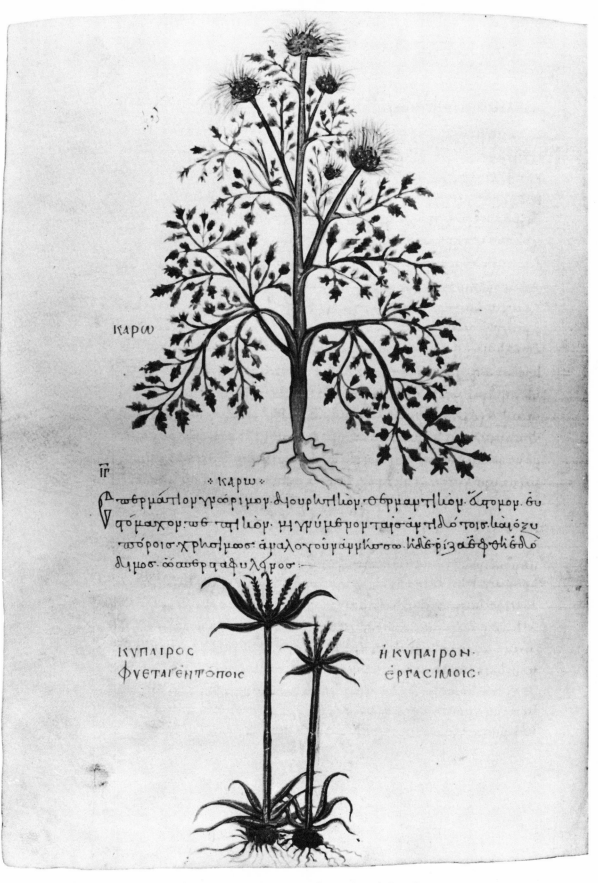

Description of pennywort in a tenth-century Greek manuscript
from Constantinople

Europe at the end of the Middle Ages. Then people looked with new eyes at the old manuscripts which had survived from the Greeks and at the old and new learning that was coming from the East, and they became curious about parts of the world that were only half known or not known at all.

So man's knowledge of what the earth is like and how to sail the seas began to grow. From the North African Moors, Europeans learned something about Africa, and from looking at the maps drawn by the great map makers of the time, they began to think about the possibilities of travel by sea. In the fifteenth century in Portugal, Prince Henry the Navigator, who was both a prince and a great scientist, gathered around him men of every kind who were interested in astronomy and navigation. In ship after ship, Prince Henry sent men out onto the Atlantic to search for new islands, to study winds and currents, and to work their way down the West African coast to shores to which no Europeans had ever sailed before. These men, among whom Columbus spent some time, knew of the earlier Viking voyages to Greenland and already

knew that the earth is round, though they did not know as yet how large the earth is. The explorations of the fifteenth and six-teenth centuries down and around the coast of Africa, to the New World, and at last around the whole globe brought Europeans in contact with enormous numbers of new things—new plants, new animals, and new peoples.

Meanwhile, in the sixteenth century a new star was discovered, and the old idea that there are only a fixed number of stars was shaken. Then, in 1608, the telescope was invented and a few years later, the microscope. Using these two instruments, men discovered

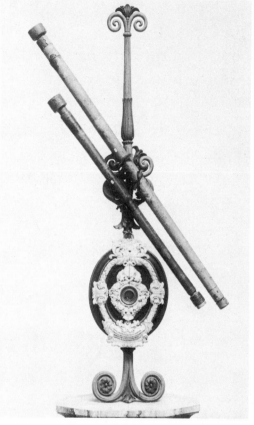

A modern 48-inch schmidt telescope and two of Galileo's telescopes

with amazement both that the universe was infinitely greater than anyone had suspected and that right around them there was another universe of things too tiny to be seen with the naked eye. Within a few years, even though men like Kepler and Galileo were punished for their extraordinary ideas about new stars, new planets, and the motion of the earth, scholars and all sorts of people from one end of Europe to the other were scanning the heavens with telescopes and peering through microscopes at "the little animals in a drop of water"; and in these same years people not only were reading about but also traveling to the new places so recently discovered.

All these new things excited people's imagination and set them thinking in new ways. Finding new plants and animals put the familiar ones in a new light. Scholars began to classify and name groups of them and tried to work out a systematic theory to explain both the similarities within a group (for instance, among all the creatures we call birds) and the differences (for instance, between an eagle, a canary, a robin, a sea gull, and an ostrich, which cannot fly).

Observing, recording, and observing so as to fit plants and animals into groups or to map out and understand the universe, men became better and more acute observers. Other men, looking at the earth itself, began to have definite ideas about the earth's age and about creatures that were known through fossils and often were found in strange places, as when fossilized sea creatures were found on mountain tops, showing that where now there were mountains once a sea had been. The Greeks had already begun to think about the earth and had wondered about fossils, but their ideas had not been followed up. At the turn of the nineteenth century, scientists put together their own observations and began to build a new theory about the earth's age. Then a Frenchman, Boucher de Perthes, recognized as man-made tools certain of the stones that were found together with fossilized animals, and he realized that man must be much older than anyone had believed. Yet with all the interest in exploration, observation, and experiment there was very little scientific study of man.

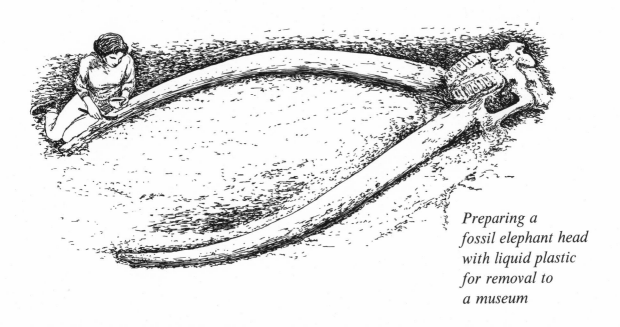

Preparing a fossil elephant head with liquid plastic for removal to a museum

Some knowledge of man's body had been accumulating since ancient times. However, as observations of the inside of the body had to be made after people were dead, real knowledge of physiology, or the way a living body works, did not develop until long after anatomy, the structure of the body, was quite well-known. In the fourth century B.C. Aristotle recognized that the blood flows in the veins, and in the second century A.D. Galen recognized that it also flows in the arteries. But a full grasp of how the blood moves, with the heart as the pump, came only in 1628, when William Harvey published his study of the circulation of the blood.

Artists, too, had been learning about the human body as they made studies for statues and paintings. In the Notebooks of the great Italian artist Leonardo da Vinci, who died in 1519, we find side by side sketches for paintings of madonnas, studies of muscles in the human body, and designs for machines—even flying machines. Still, as far as man was concerned, this thinking had to do with the structure and working of his body—how an arm moved in its socket—not with the relations of human beings to one another.

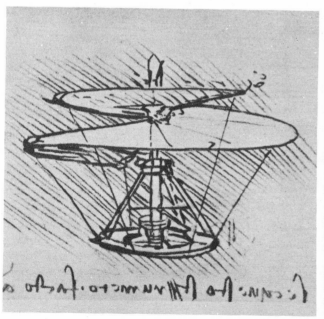 

da Vinci's design for an aerial screw and a scale model of it

*Studies of facial expression
at various ages, by
Leonardo da Vinci*

But though a real science of man is very young, attempts to think systematically about man have a long history. In the fifth century B.C. the Greek historian Herodotus wrote an account of some of the peoples known to the Greeks. In the fourth century B.C. the Greek philosopher Plato tried to think out how children should be brought up to become citizens of the most perfect society he could imagine. But the study of man was not yet a science. For another two thousand years, travelers told stories about the strange behavior of faraway peoples, and few men thought these tales had anything to do with themselves. Marveling at what they heard, Europeans could still think, "I am so different. What these people do has nothing to do with me."

But from the time when Prince Henry the Navigator sent his ships down the coast of Africa, the explorers' careful descriptions of the natural world included descriptions of human beings. When in the eighteenth century Captain Cook was sent to explore the Pacific, he brought back not only observations of the stars and descriptions of ocean currents, maps of coast lines, and samples of new plants, but also descriptions of the savages who inhabited the islands he discovered. Earlier, when missionaries were sent from Europe, scholars and religious men discussed the problem of whether Africans or American Indians had souls which could be saved. Very practical problems also made Europeans want to know more about distant peoples. In North America traders of the

Hudson's Bay Company explored new territories to find Indians who could be persuaded to become fur trappers. In West Africa, when the British were trying to stop the slave trade, businessmen wanted to know what trade substitutes could be found for slaves. So in 1817 they sent a young Englishman, Thomas Bowdich, inland from the coast to visit the Ashanti, a great warrior people who were also slave traders. Bowdich wrote the first full account of how the Ashanti lived.

But though many of the men who looked at these new peoples were good observers and recorders, they were not trying to learn about other peoples in order to fit them into a theory of how life began or how the human mind works. Few people realized that

these others were human beings like ourselves, able to learn what we can learn, savage only because they did not have our history.

Modern anthropology began when men or women, specially trained at universities, could say of primitive peoples whom they went out to study, "These are human beings like myself. Though they know nothing about writing or higher mathematics or the natural sciences or the great religions, the differences between what they are and what I am have come about because of what I was able to learn in a highly civilized country and what they were able to learn in a little faraway society. But they, too, have a culture, a way of life. They marry and bring up their children. They know how to find food and how to keep order and how to give their children some idea of what man is. If I want to understand them, I must respect them and respect their culture." Respecting a primitive people does not mean that the anthropologist must give up everything that has been gained in thousands of years of civilization. It does mean that he must believe that each people is struggling to find ways for human beings to live together and that he must respect their efforts.

There are other reasons, too, why the study of the stars and of insects came earlier than the study of man. It is much more difficult to study something that is the same size as oneself than it is to study something that is either very much bigger or very much smaller than oneself. Generation after generation of men can observe the same sun and write down what they have seen for the next generation to read. But human beings, whether they are scientists or the people in whom scientists are interested, live only one human generation. A biologist can bring up many generations of white rats and see how the present generation resemble their great-great-grandfathers, and the same scientist will also see this generation's many-times-grandchildren. Generations of fruit flies are even easier to study, for a fruit fly lives its whole life in a little more than a month. Also, one scientist can watch a whole cage of rats at once, or a jar with dozens of fruit flies in it. It is harder to study human beings, for they take as long to grow up and they live as long as the person studying them, and they move about at the same speed as he does.

The feelings human beings have about themselves and other human beings also made it difficult for men to learn how to study mankind. Every people in the world have ideas about what human beings are, where the soul comes from and where it is going to, what the difference is between being alive and being dead, between being a male and being a female, between being a child and being an adult; and these ideas become part of religious beliefs. But whenever scientists begin to study any subject, they are sure to find out something which was not known before, and almost always some of the new facts do not fit into the old theories. Then those

who care very much about what people believe—especially the priests and prophets and teachers, the generals and governors and kings, whose duty it is to worry about what people believe— begin to worry for fear that a change in one bit of knowledge will upset all the rest.

In the seventeenth century, the astronomers' discoveries that the earth turns on its axis and revolves around the sun (instead of the sun revolving around the earth) and that there were other planets and moons and stars never seen before were very upsetting ideas to the educated world. The earlier knowledge scholars had built up about the heavens had become woven together with the religious theory of creation and then, when the knowledge of the universe was enlarged, people felt that all their beliefs were shaken. Nevertheless, even though a man like Galileo was punished for spreading the new knowledge, Europeans quickly learned to explore the universe with their new instruments, and slowly they learned also that the new knowledge of our solar system need not affect their faith. Today it is so well understood that a change in knowledge about the universe is not irreligious that the keepers of man's faith can bless space exploration as once they blessed the ships that went to sea.

Much the same thing happened when scientists began to look systematically at rock formations and at fossils and realized that it was necessary to work out a new theory about the age of the earth and about how old life is on the earth. Again people were disturbed until they learned to see that it was possible to change their ideas about how *long* it took for birds and fish and animals and, finally, man to appear, without upsetting their beliefs about the creation of the world.

The study of man himself had to begin even more carefully. When, in 1858, Charles Darwin suggested that men as we know them today have developed as other species of living creatures have developed, there was great consternation and much worry. For if what he said was true, the creation of men themselves must have taken much longer than anyone then believed.

Because people do feel so strongly about their beliefs, it is necessary when we are studying human beings to be very careful of their feelings. But this is not easy. Even today we are only beginning to know something about how people do feel. How to be careful of people's feelings is also a scientific problem.

Another reason why it is hard to study man is that it is difficult to do real experiments with human beings. If someone wants to see if it is true that a certain kind of fertilizer makes more beans grow, he can put the fertilizer on one half of his experimental garden and not on the other half. Then even if more beans grow in the fertilized part of the garden, no one need feel sorry for the unfertilized part where the beans grew less well. What we want to know is how to get bigger or tenderer or earlier-ripening beans for eating. No one needs to think about the beans' feelings. Nor need anyone fear that such an experiment will turn the gardener into a cruel man.

When we come to human beings it is quite different. For if we know that a certain kind of food is really good for babies, we cannot prevent some of them from having the food for the sake of an experiment. Before we give new foods or vitamins or medicines to children, we first make very careful experiments with animals to be sure that the untried thing is good and safe. For instance, the main experimental work that led to a safe and effective vaccine against polio was done with chimpanzees. Then, when it was certain that the vaccine was safe, it was given to a limited number of children whose parents were willing to have them take part in an experiment to show how well it protected human beings. Finally, when it was clear that the vaccine had protected these children, it was used generally to protect the lives of children and adults in the United States, as well as many other countries.

With human beings we can only make very limited experiments. We cannot ask a group of tall men to marry short girls or a group of brown-eyed men to marry blue-eyed girls so that we can find out how many of their children will be tall or short, brown-eyed or blue-eyed. Nor can we make experiments to see whether by punishing children or not punishing them we can make them grow up differently. We had to find some other way.

Other ways of studying man opened up when scientists recognized that modern man, *Homo sapiens,* is one species regardless of whether he is an Eskimo, an Ashanti, a Frenchman, a Balinese, or an American. When we knew this, we could say that the differences between our behavior and the behavior of these other peoples—who talk and walk and think so differently from us—must come about because of what each generation learns. We could see what this would mean. An Eskimo baby who was brought up by American parents would speak English, hate castor oil, and act like any other American child; and an American baby who was brought up by an Eskimo family would grow up to be a seal hunter, to like eating blubber, and to speak Eskimo.

When this was clear, we were really able to start studying human beings. To do so, we had to travel to places where people lived very differently from ourselves, study their lives, and record everything about them very carefully. This has been our substitute for making experiments on human beings: studying people already living in very different ways in very different parts of the world.

In this way, we study what a people *have* done, what they *have* thought best for their children or for their citizens. Then, when we have made several such studies, we can compare the ways of two peoples who live quite differently from each other. We can look at the Eskimo, who live almost entirely on animals and fish, and we can look at the Balinese, who live almost entirely on rice and vegetables, and we can begin to find out something about the kind of diet human beings really need. Or if we want to find out if it is true, as some people have said, that human beings always make war, we can look around the world at other peoples to find out whether there are any peoples who have brought up their children without a knowledge of war. If we do find such a people—the Eskimo, for instance, who know about quarrels between two persons but not about organized fights between two groups—then without making any new experiments we can say that human beings will *not* always, in all circumstances, go to war. Without knowing it, the Eskimo have made the experiment for us.

But until we had learned that all the peoples now on the earth belong to one species and live differently from one another not because they look different but because they have learned different things, we could not think of their ways of life as experiments in living.

There is still another reason why we have only very slowly begun to study man, and that is the need for special tools. Every

Finnish dock worker

Camayura Indian of Brazil

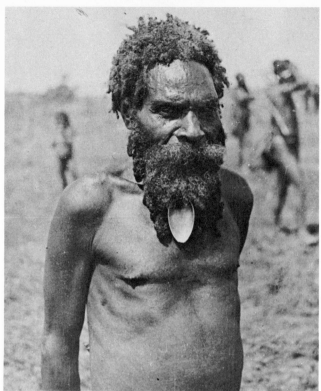

Yugoslav farmer   *Native of New Guinea*

science has to invent special tools before much work can be done. Of course, we can begin to explore with our eyes and our hands and our hearing, our sense of taste and smell. But no science was possible until people could keep records, until observers could write down notes for themselves or for others to read and use later. Both the Mesopotamians and the Egyptians developed forms of writing with which they could record what they saw when they watched the stars and the ideas which grew out of their watching. In the New World, also, the Mayan people of Yucatan, Guatemala, and Honduras—whose civilization was dying out at the time of the Spanish conquest—were among the world's great early astronomers, and they too had developed a form of writing, which we know mainly from the inscriptions they carved on tall stone pillars.

As each science developed, new tools were invented. With the invention of the telescope, astronomy became a very different subject; when people could see the mountains on the moon and the stars in the Milky Way, there was no longer room for disagreement about what the moon and the Milky Way were, and scientists could go on to study new problems. So too, the microscope opened up a new world to scientists, who with this instrument could see the inside of a seed or a spore on a fern as it grew. But there are enormous differences between the earliest telescopes and microscopes and those which scientists have today. With his best telescope Galileo discovered the satellites of Jupiter and the mountains of the moon. With modern astronomical telescopes, it is possible to see galaxies in outer space, beyond our own galactic system; and now, since the invention of radio-astronomy, it is possible to hear "radio-stars" so distant they cannot yet be seen.

When it came to studying human beings, we needed to study peoples who lived in the Arctic and in the tropics, on mountains and by the sea, in tiny tribes and in great kingdoms, those who knew nothing about reading and writing, and others who had

Chinese official in Imperial Court dress

Kenya doctor

kept records for thousands of years. We could not point telescopes at them to watch them, nor could we put them all together in a giant glass jar to watch them as fruit flies are watched. We had no instruments to look inside them to see what happened in their brains when they tried to solve a problem or in their blood stream when they were angry or frightened. We could not cut open a man who was frightened to see what his stomach looked like. Nor could we get left-handed men to marry left-handed girls or color-blind men to marry color-blind girls to find out whether their children would be left-handed or color-blind.

This meant that the first scientists who seriously started to study human beings had to use themselves as if they were tools. A man cannot tell by watching a deer or a mouse how the deer or the mouse really feels; he can only say that the deer runs away or that the mouse cowers against the wall. But a man watching another man can understand something about how he feels, and if he learns the other man's language, he can ask him questions and listen to his answers. So the study of human beings in many parts of the world began with men and women, trained to be anthropologists, who asked questions. At first they tried talking and listening through interpreters, people who knew something about both languages, but this did not work out very well. The interpreters themselves often did not understand the questions and the answers, and so everyone was likely to get mixed up. To understand what really was meant, anthropologists had to learn the language the people spoke.

There are several problems about learning the language of a primitive tribe which you might not think of right away. The first thing an anthropologist has to expect is that the new language will be quite different from European languages. That is, the differences between the new language and English will be greater than those between, say, English and French and Latin, or

English and German and Norwegian, or English and Russian, because all these languages belong to the same family. When we are just beginning to learn the language of an unknown primitive people, we do not know whether it will be the kind in which one syllable after another can be linked together to make something longer than an English sentence or whether it will be the kind in which there are only short words which always stand by themselves. We do not know whether the language will make the kinds of differences ours does when we use *she* to talk about a girl, and *he* to talk about a boy, and *it* to talk about a stick. In languages like ours one can say: "*He* hit *her* with *it*." But in some other languages the same sentence would be: "*Third person* hit *third person* with *third person*." Still other languages make more differences than we do, as they have special pronouns not only for males and females and things but also for long things and round things and hollow things. We do not know whether the word for two of something will be different from the word for one of that thing, and if it is, whether the difference will be like that between *cat* and *cats,* or *mouse* and *mice,* or *ox* and *oxen.* We do not know whether the same words can be used for men and sheep and eggs or whether different words have to be used, such as a *crowd of men,* a *flock of sheep,* a *clutch of eggs,* a *pride of lions,* a *swarm of bees,* or a *covey of quail.* We do not even know whether what we call the "parts of speech"—such as nouns and pronouns, verbs, adjectives and adverbs—will be anything like those in English.

When I was studying anthropology, I was prepared to learn languages which no one—except for the people who spoke them —had ever tried to learn systematically by studying samples of various languages which were already known. My teacher, Professor Franz Boas, had studied the languages of the Indians of western Canada and of the Eskimo, and he gave us examples of how these languages worked. Here is an Eskimo song that goes with a game:

Igdluaquāpik!	*qailaurit*	*patalaugluk*
Dear partner!	come,	let us two strike (with our palms)
patatalaugluk	*pataqtualaugluk*	*igdlukitaqatalaugluk!*
let us two go on striking (with our palms)	let us two strike very hard (with our palms),	let us two play ball together!*

From this song you can see that Eskimo is a language in which one bit after another is added on to change the meaning of a word.

When an anthropologist arrives among the primitive people he wants to study, he must find someone who can interpret at least a little, so that he can ask what people call things and how they ask questions and ask other people to do things. Probably no one there will have any ideas about what a word or a sentence is; nor will anyone know that their language has a grammar. They know how to speak it and how to correct children when they make mistakes. So the anthropologist must behave partly like a child who is being taught to speak and partly like the first person who made a grammar; and he must patiently collect a great many sentences: "I see a man, I see a woman, I see a dog; I see it (a woman), I see it (a man), I see it (a dog)," on and on, until he can both speak the language and write down its grammar.

While he is doing this he must also learn people's names, and where they live, and how they spend their time, and what the rules are which he must be careful not to break. Then he must find

*From Franz Boas' "The Eskimo of Baffin Land and Hudson Bay," *Bulletin of the American Museum of Natural History*, Vol. 15 (1901), Part 1, p. 347. By permission of the publishers.

two or three people who enjoy talking—people who do not mind answering thousands of questions about things that seem perfectly natural to them, such as why animals from the sea and animals from the land may not be eaten on the same day, or why it is a bad thing to walk on the roads at high noon, or why children may not shout and play in a tent where a sacred pipe is kept. These people who enjoy talking and explaining things—anthropologists call them "informants"—become partners in the work of trying to understand all about the life of the tribe.

As he works, the anthropologist writes down hundreds of pages of notes and makes little sketches showing how a bird is snared, or how a fish trap is made and used, or where the different

Balinese children teaching the author their language

Indian bands set up their tents when a whole tribe meet for the summer buffalo hunt, or how people play string games on their fingers. When someone takes sick, the anthropologist must find out why people think the sick person got that way. Was it because he was hurt by black magic, or because he broke a rule, or was a ghost trying to kill him, or is the sickness a sign that he will become a holy man?

As far as possible, the anthropologist tries to get close to people. A man anthropologist goes hunting and fishing with the men; a woman anthropologist holds the babies on her lap and strings beads or flowers or makes baskets. The anthropologist learns to eat all sorts of unfamiliar foods—dragonflies, octopus, blubber. He learns to sit in new positions which he may find very uncomfortable—cross-legged or squatting on one heel. All these things make it possible to understand the people better. Because he and they are the same kind of living human beings, when he uses his legs—which are just like theirs—as they use theirs, he finds out more about how they feel as they move.

This method of studying another people is one-sided. The anthropologist understands a great many things about the savages which they do not understand themselves. But at the same time he can never feel exactly as they do, of course, and even though he speaks the language quite well, it is not his own language, his mother tongue in which he was sung to sleep when he was a baby. Also, although many of the savages may become good friends who spend long hours helping him—dictating stories slowly so he can write them down, patiently explaining just how one man is related to another—they do not understand what scientific work is.

This difficulty disappears as peoples in remote parts of the world begin to learn something about the modern world, see machines, and learn about writing and medicine. And when we study a people who are modern like ourselves, they can learn very quickly what it means to think about their own way of life —to think about it carefully as they would think about the life of another people or the life of birds.

You might try the experiment of describing your house and your street and all the people who live there and how they treat each other, as if you were talking to someone from another planet who knew nothing at all about the world. If you were doing this, you would not be able to say: "We have a new-model Ford in the garage." You would have to describe what an automobile is, and how cars are made by groups of people who are gathered together to make them in work places filled with special machinery, called factories, and how the cars are named after the company which makes them, and how a different-looking car—called a "model" —is designed and built each year. Then you would have to explain what a garage is, and what it means to park a car, and how people feel about old cars and new cars and cars bought second-hand. You would have to explain what it means to "turn in" a car and why some people make a hobby—and you would have to tell him what a "hobby" is—of very old cars or small foreign cars. If you had to explain everything in words or, if you are good at drawing, with little sketches, you can see how long it would take; even so the stranger would not understand very much about what you were telling him.

Yet this is the way the first anthropologists had to work. There were no cameras that could be taken to the field, and moving pictures and tape recorders had not been invented. Nor had typewriters been invented. If an anthropologist worried for fear all his notes might be lost, he had to make extra copies by hand. So he could bring back only his notes and his memories of what he had seen and heard. If he knew how to draw, he could make sketches. If he was musical, he could try to write down the music, using the notes invented for European music. His success in recording the language depended on whether his ear was sensitive enough to pick up sounds which did not exist in his language. A war dance, the movements of a hunter in the bush, whistling sounds imitating the call of a bird—these could not really be described at all.

In the last twenty-five years all this has changed. Now an anthropologist has special tools as important as the telescope and the microscope. The camera was invented long before, but with earlier cameras only carefully posed pictures could be taken. Then came the modern still camera with which it is possible to take pictures at long distances or very close up, and with great speed, and also modern film which can be used in almost any light. And now we also have the moving-picture camera and the tape

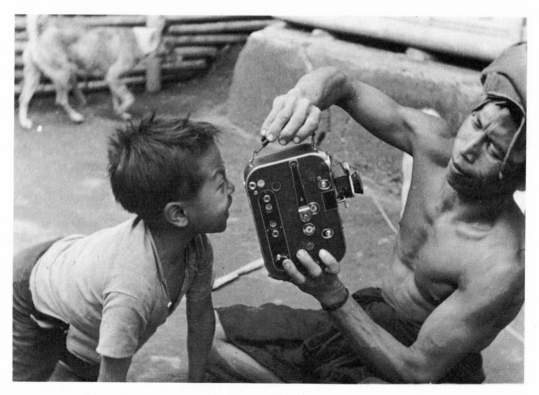

A movie camera is an object of curiosity to many Balinese

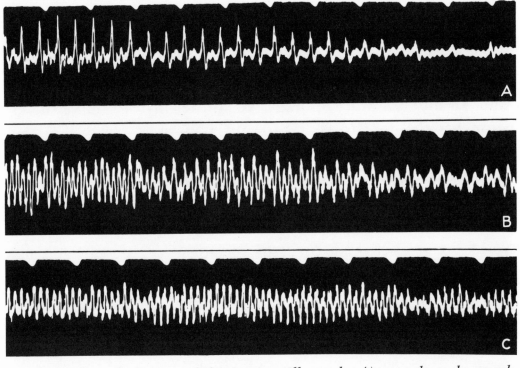

Sound waves can be recorded on an oscillograph. A) records male speech, B) is a male solo with orchestral accompaniment, C) is a dance orchestra. (frequency of timing wave at top of each oscillogram is 60 cycles)

recorder. Of course, it it still important for the anthropologist to use the fact that he is himself a human being like the people he is studying. The tape recorder cannot learn the language for him; the moving-picture camera cannot make friends with anyone. But now for the first time he can bring back for other scientists to see and hear—and for himself to look at and listen to again and again—something that happened only once on a faraway island. As the microscope made it possible to see things too small for the naked eye and the telescope things too far away for the naked eye, film and tape make it possible to catch and keep more sights and sounds than the brain can take in and sort at one time.

So, today films of how people walk and hunt, dance and make speeches, learn and teach, and tape recordings which give all the fine shadings no one can write down have become the anthropologists' substitutes for experiments. In experiments, the scientist can do the same thing over and over—add one chemical to another, shut fruit flies up together under special conditions, graft the limb of one kind of pear tree onto a branch of another kind. In modern anthropology we still let history make the experiments for us, but we record them in such a way that they can be studied over and over. As our ideas grow and change, we can test the new ones out against the old films and the old tape recordings long after the people who were filmed and recorded have deserted their old ways and have come into the modern world. Just as petrified fossils of old forms of life can give new information to the paleontologist who studies them, so old films of a forgotten way of life can continue to give us new information and help us to test out new theories. But we must make these records as quickly as possible, before the last primitive peoples of the world have become partly civilized and have lost their old ways.

Furthermore, if we really want to use our knowledge of how other peoples have solved the problems of living at different times, in different climates, using different tools, and sharing different beliefs, we must look at the way one particular people—a tribe of Eskimo or Indians or Africans—live. It is not enough for us to have scattered bits of knowledge about many other peoples, to know that some people hunt with bows and arrows while others use spears, that some catch their game in traps while others set the prairie on fire or surround a whole herd of buffalo or reindeer. It is not enough to know that some people live in snow houses, some in tents and some in caves, some in houses made of rice paper and some in modern steel-constructed apartment buildings. It is not enough to know that some people try to get the kind of weather they want by using magical charms or by climbing high up in tall palm trees to "cut the fingers of the wind," while others try to deserve good weather by leading good lives, still others put on masks and dance for rain, and we ourselves have engineers who "seed" the clouds. All these scattered details are very interesting, of course. It makes a difference if when you look at a piece of long-range artillery, you realize that the principle on which it is based developed in part from the idea of the blowgun with which primitive people in Malaya killed monkeys and birds. You look at a stairway from a new point of view when you realize what a big invention people made when they learned how to build two-story houses and how to support a great vaulted ceiling without pillars. You understand better how men have learned to think about how their crops, their houses, and their children may be affected by the way they themselves behave and by the way they approach the supernatural powers which they believe guide and protect them.

But if you look at human history like this, bit by bit, and know a little about weapons and a little about houses and a little about magic, you will never learn how all these things fit together in the way of life—what we call the "culture"—of a particular people. Really to understand a culture we must know all about a people —where they live, what they eat and where they get their food, what kind of families they have, how they bring up their children, how they see the world, and how they treat strangers and new ideas.

HOW

SOME

PEOPLES

LIVE

The Eskimo

THE Eskimo live on the northernmost margin of the New World,
along the coasts and on the peninsulas and islands of the Arctic
Sea, above the line where trees will grow. They have learned how
to live in a world where in the farthest north there are four months
when the sun doesn't rise above the horizon, and there are but two
months when the sun shines the day around and there are no
frosts. Though the weather is milder on the Canadian coast than
on the islands of the High Arctic, the time when the waters are
open, when the shores are free of ice, when gay flowers bloom, and
the air is filled with the cries of birds is everywhere short. During most of the year the Eskimo live very close to danger—
danger of being caught in blinding storms, danger of being ma-
rooned on breaking sea ice, danger of starving to death when
wild weather keeps the hunters home. Then they live so close to

97

death that they cannot afford to care for their old people, who themselves ask to be allowed to die rather than become a burden on the group. The dogs that pull the sledges are precious as life, for without them hunters can move only a little distance in winter; yet sometimes people have to choose between death and eating their dogs. In a disaster they may have to choose between cannibalism and death. No people we know about face a harder life, a life that requires more continuous alertness, bravery, and fortitude.

Yet the Eskimo are also an exceedingly cheerful, jolly, hopeful, and hospitable people. Even though it is hard work to get food, they welcome visitors. Even though traveling is dangerous, especially when just one family travels alone for many weeks across frozen wastes, the Eskimo travel a great deal, sometimes on trips that take several years. Even though finding food—seals or walruses, bears or whales, reindeer or fish or birds—is something they have to think about almost all the time, you would never guess that they were worried if you came into a snow house in the evening after a day of good hunting. For then, coming in from the cold and dark, you would find half the people of the settlement crowded on the platforms, small babies and puppies crawling about among the visitors, the air warmed, and the arched walls lighted by the lamps. The men might be gambling, throwing little carved ivory animals for dice. Some women might be trying out tongue twisters, each shouting louder and faster than the one before. Others might be making string figures. Or everyone might be listening to a storyteller, each one eating a delicious bit of frozen meat cut off from a chunk as it was passed from hand to hand.

There are many interesting things about the Eskimo—how they build their snow houses, how they dress, how they travel

with their teams of fierce dogs, how they hunt on the sea in a kayak, the little skin canoe into which a man's body fits like a stopper. But perhaps most interesting of all is the way human beings have learned to live together under such very difficult conditions, and all their lives keep up the hard fight against cold and famine and disaster.

There are in all about 50,000 Eskimo who live in the great stretch of land between Greenland and the Bering Sea, not in every part of this vast area, but wherever it is possible to get a living from the sea and the shore, the rivers and lakes and tree-less plains. Starting from Greenland and making his way across Canada or else across the northern islands to Alaska, an Eskimo could speak his own language all the way. However, as he moved from one little tribe to another he would find many differences in the way people live. But he would also find much that was familiar. In general, he would know how to hunt. He would know what to do when a whole settlement joined together to drive a great herd of reindeer into a narrow valley or into a stream or pond where hunters waited to spear the animals. He would know how to move on ice so that to a seal basking near its hole he would look like another seal. He would know how to hunt down sea birds when they were losing their summer feathers and could swim and dive but could not fly away. He would know how to set his team of dogs jumping and snapping at a polar bear until he could move in and spear it. But he would realize that this was not enough. If he was to be successful, he would have to learn about the exact conditions of land and sea and ice in each place. If he traveled far from home, it would not be enough for him to know how to make out of driftwood the kind of harpoon shaft or bow used by his little tribe. For after he had traveled a thousand miles, his har-poon shaft might break or his bow be lost. Then, if there was no driftwood, he would have to make a new harpoon shaft or a new

bow out of reindeer antler in the way the people he was visiting made theirs.

In every place where a group of Eskimo go to hunt or to fish, to catch seals or to find polar bears when each bear is wandering by itself in the snow, it is necessary to know exactly what to expect and what to do. In the far north of Greenland, hunters must cache away enough frozen food to carry their families through the darkest winter months, when no hunting is possible. When a sudden freeze catches walruses on the ice, hunters must be prepared to dash out after them, before the animals find a place to slip back into the water. And people must always know when and where it is safe to live as well as to hunt on the frozen sea.

Every Eskimo boy learns to hunt and fish, to manage a dog team, to make a kayak and a sledge, to make his own tools and his own weapons—harpoons and spears and bows—and to build a snow house all by himself. In fact, every Eskimo boy learns to do everything that every man does except talk to the spirits. And every Eskimo girl learns to do everything that every Eskimo woman does: to dress skins and to make clothes and boots and tents, to prepare meat and cook, to take care of the children, and in an emergency to do the things that a man does. The toys children play with are miniatures of the very things that men and women use for work.

A man and his wife—or wives—make a complete team, each necessary to the other. The man makes the wooden frame of his hunting kayak, but the skin cover is made by the woman. The woman fashions the skin tent in which the family lives in the short summer, and it is hers; but the man must give her the skins for it, and he makes and owns the tent poles. The man makes the bone needles the woman needs for sewing. He also makes out of soapstone the lamp and pot the woman must have for cooking. But after he has made these things, they belong to her alone.

All the tasks which in modern America are divided up among thousands of people can there be done easily by a man and his

wife, and they can teach the necessary skills to their children. Nevertheless, because of the traveling and the visiting and because of the danger to the whole family if a hunter is unlucky, or if one of a couple gets hurt or takes sick or dies, people need more than one family for protection against hunger and cold and loneliness.

So people live in settlements of perhaps ten or twenty families —seldom more than a hundred people altogether—and call themselves "the people of such-and-such a place." But they do not always stay together, for only at some seasons of the year is there enough food or the right kind of hunting to support the whole group. At other times, families must scatter. And every year settlements change a little, as some people go off to live elsewhere and others decide to join the group. In each little settlement there is one hunter who is luckier—for that is what people say—than all the others. As long as his luck continues, people depend on him and take his advice about when to start one kind of hunting or when to move inland. But if anyone disagrees with "the man who knows everything best," one of the names for a leader, nothing prevents the one who disagrees from going his own way. There are no chiefs of any kind, just stronger men and weaker ones, luckier hunters and less lucky ones, and in every settlement

there are one or two men or women, called "angakut," who have learned to talk to the spirits to discover why some trouble has come upon people—what has become of a lost object, why storms rage, why no animals are caught, why someone has become sick or has died.

Though we do not yet know exactly where the Eskimo came from nor when the first Eskimo came into Alaska, they have lived in the Arctic for at least 2,000 years and perhaps much longer. Their name for themselves is *Inuit,* which means simply "people." The name "Eskimo," from an Indian word meaning "raw-meat eaters," was given to them by Europeans.

The Old Norse sagas about the earliest settlements in Greenland in the eleventh century tell of the "skraellings" whom the Norsemen found there. These were perhaps Eskimo, and if so, they were the first people discovered by Europeans in the New World. Yet no one knows exactly, for the Norse settlements died out. But since the sixteenth century, explorers and fishermen, traders and whalers and missionaries of many nations, moving into the Arctic from east and west, have discovered groups of Eskimo. The Eskimo began trading for muskets and metal, but except that hunting became easier, their life changed little and slowly. However, explorers and scientists have given us accounts of their methods of hunting before they had guns and iron for knives and harpoon points, and archaeologists have dug up sites where Eskimo lived long ago. So we know something about how they lived before they met Europeans and how for 2,000 years they have wandered back and forth on the Arctic shores.

So today it is possible to get a good picture of how these people, without metal, without any way of dividing up jobs except between men and women, and with only the simplest ways of organizing a group to live together, have kept alive in the cold, snowy north. In this chapter, we shall talk particularly about the Central Eskimo, whom Franz Boas visited in 1883–1884.

This painting of West Greenland Eskimo, executed in 1654,
is the first known picture of these people

We know, of course, that the Eskimo came from somewhere else and could have moved into the far north only gradually, because they needed to have so many things before they could go there at all. First there are the things that human beings had to have before they could live where it was cold. They had to know how to make fire, how to hunt and fish for the creatures that live in the cold, how to travel about, how to make clothes to protect them from the cold outdoors, and how to build houses to keep them warm indoors. These are all things which Siberians, who live across Bering Strait, and also those Indians who live just south of the Eskimo had to know, too. In fact, Indians used some things which the Eskimo did not—snowshoes, for example, which are good for walking on soft snow but are useless on rough ice or on snow frozen hard as ice. Human beings have never lived in Antarctica, but the penguins who go there in the summertime have some of the same problems of living that the Eskimo have in the Arctic.

If you picture the ancestors of the Eskimo venturing farther and farther north for short trips before they could live there all year round, you can see how the perfectly adapted clothes and houses and tools began to develop. Shoes would be necessary, not just sandals or moccasins but thick, warm boots that protect the whole leg. Trousers for both men and women were essential; a short skirt or a breechclout would not be enough. The materials from which clothing was made had to be windproof and waterproof, something from which snow could be brushed off before it melted and then froze again. Mittens were needed to cover the hands, and hoods to cover the head and ears. People had to learn how to keep warm by dressing in layers and in clothes made loosely enough so that air could circulate inside and dry up the sweat that would otherwise first dampen their clothes and then make them stiff

with frost. It was necessary also to find some way to protect a
little baby completely.

Although styles of clothing vary from one group to another,
all the Eskimo have solved these problems. So, for instance, the
woman's jacket is made with extra fullness in the back so a baby
can ride inside it, warm and safe; a girdle at the waist keeps the
baby from slipping down. Also the woman's hood is made large
and loose so that a baby, peering over his mother's shoulder, is
covered and yet can see out into the world. Even the clothing of
the carved wooden dolls with which little girls play is made in
this fashion.

It is interesting to notice, too, that there are problems which
the Eskimo did not solve. They invented eye protectors, flat strips
of bone or wood into which narrow slits were cut, to lessen the
glare of sun on snow and ice. But they have no means of protecting the cornea of the eye from freezing, which sometimes happens
in a snowstorm or on icy water. They have boots and mittens,
but in some of the costumes there are gaps—more than are
needed for ventilation—around the waist where the jacket doesn't
quite meet the trousers or in the middle of the thigh where a
woman's leggings do not quite meet her short trousers. These
exposed places gradually turn black, and when people take off
their clothes, their skin is striped.

After clothes, the next most important invention was a proper
house. Whether it is dug partly out of the earth or out of deep
snow, whether it is made partly of stone or of snow or of skin,
the house must keep people warm enough so they can eat and
sleep without danger of freezing when they are not moving about.
It must be ventilated so that people will not suffocate and so that
the lamps will burn. It must be warm enough and yet if it is built
of snow, not so warm that the snow will melt. Because fuel is

*Eskimo
toys*

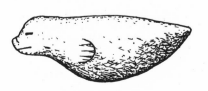

scarce, the house has to be built so as to make the best use of a little heat. For the Eskimo who live in snow houses one of the hard times of year is in between seasons—in spring when the snow roof of the house begins to melt but it is not yet warm enough to move into a summer tent, and in autumn when it is very cold but there is not yet enough snow to cut snow blocks for a house.

Every detail of the building and arrangement of a snow house is worked out very carefully, whether it is a tiny shelter built in an hour for one hunter for one night or a large house built in half a day and shared by two families for a month or more. Often two men work together. One stays outside and cuts snow blocks while the other is inside, fitting the blocks together in a spiral until at last, when he raises the key block into the top of the dome, he is entirely enclosed. Then he cuts his way out the side. Afterward he adds on the tunnellike passage that keeps out the wind

and, sloping down a little from the inner entrance, keeps the warmer air inside. Storage lockers are built onto the passage and open in or out, depending on their use. Sometimes neighbors join up passages so they can visit without going out of doors. Before anyone comes into the passage, he takes off his outer jacket, brushes it off with a special snow beater, and stows it away to keep it dry and safe from the hungry dogs.

The problem of fire for light, warmth and cooking, and for drying clothes was solved by burning oil from blubber in a soapstone lamp that serves all these purposes at once. North of the tree line there is only brush in summer and the fat of seals or whales in winter to serve as fuel. Soapstone itself is scarce, and sometimes people must travel for a year to find it. Then, just as they barter for scarce things with their neighbors, they "barter" with the rock and leave presents near the place where they dig out the precious soapstone. All her life a woman carries her soap-

stone lamp and pot with her, and when she dies they are placed
near her grave.

Two families or one family with two women live in each house.
As each woman has her own fire on one of the two side platforms,
the house is warmed by two lamps (and sometimes by another
little one on the bed in back and a fourth in front near the entrance). Hunters have small lamps to carry with them when they
travel away from home. If a stranger comes alone to visit, his
host may lend him one of his wives. Then, if he has everything
he needs to hunt, he may set up his own fire.

Once inside the house, people take off their clothes and hang
mittens and stockings to dry on racks over the lamp. Keeping
clothing dry and mended is something women have to watch
over every day. Even at those times when they are not allowed
to make anything new, they can mend worn clothes. Skins have
to be chewed to make them supple or to get them soft again;
when people are starving they may eat their clothes.

With warm clothes and a kind of house which could be built
quickly wherever they were, people could venture into the coldest

Arctic. But to hunt they needed a means of traveling quickly on snow and ice and of bringing back heavy game. To meet this need, the Eskimo have sledges and teams of dogs as independent as the people who train them. Unlike dog teams that run through woods, the Eskimo team spreads out fanwise on long traces so that the dogs may run more safely on rough snow and on thin sea ice. The leader dog, which may be a male or a female and which sets the pace and makes the other dogs behave, runs ahead on the longest lead. The younger and less trained the dog, the closer he runs to the driver, who controls them all with his voice and his long curling lash. A man without dogs cannot hope to take care of his family. So, since it takes a long time to build up a strong team and it is almost impossible to get a team to accept a strange dog, puppies are cared for as painstakingly as human infants. The children who have played and tumbled with the puppies move entirely safely among the fierce grown dogs, which have learned to hunt as well as to draw the sledge.

Just as people always have to be thinking about the weather and conditions of hunting, so too the dogs are always on their

minds. They have to be fed, though not every day. And if the dogs are not tied up, as they are throughout the summer, everything edible—meat and clothing and anything made of skins—must be stored away or put up high out of their reach. In the same way, meat or fish that can be dried or frozen to be eaten later must be stored in stone caches, to protect it not only from dogs but also from wolves, bears, foxes, and from the ravens that boldly haunt the camps, summer and winter.

The dog teams reflect the way in which small Eskimo communities are organized. As long as he remains strong the strongest man can lead the rest, and no settlement can tolerate two such men at once. When strangers from some distant tribe come into a settlement, one of them must go through a mock fight with a member of the group while the others stand about and sing. As the two men face each other, the stranger is given a terrible blow on the side of the face, which he returns—with interest. If the stranger loses the bout, he may be killed, but usually he is received as a guest and feasted instead. Within a settlement, if one man kills another, he can either go away or else stay there knowing that some day a relative of the dead man will try to kill him. Sometimes he takes over the care of the family of the man whom he has killed, waiting for someone to attack him openly or by stealth. Sometimes he may be challenged to an open fight; if the challenger loses, he too may be killed. Only when a man kills again and then again does the whole settlement turn against him and agree to let one man execute him without fear of reprisal.

The Eskimo come as close as any known people to not recognizing the difference between murder—killing a member of one's own society or, today, also the citizen of a friendly country —and other kinds of killing. However, Eskimo beliefs about the next world show that they do see a difference. For there are several different places to which people are thought to go after death. The man who has intentionally killed another man goes to the worst future world, while those who have been killed, women who have died in childbirth, and those who have drowned or frozen to death or who have died in some other terrible accident go to the best future life.

As important to a man as his sledge in winter is his kayak in summer in which he hunts on open water. Besides this light and speedy boat, the Eskimo have a large wooden-framed, skin-covered boat in which they can row or sail. This is the umiak, or woman's boat, so called because when a whole family travels in one with all their possessions, it is the women who row. However, the same boat, with an all-man crew, is also used for whaling.

With their dog sledges, the Eskimo can move on land and on the frozen sea in winter, and in their kayaks and umiaks they can travel on the water in summer. But when they move inland in summer there are also long stretches where they travel overland and can take only those possessions which they can carry on their backs or on the backs of their dogs. In their freedom of movement the Eskimo are somewhat like American families going camping for a weekend in their station wagons—with the difference: Americans take food with them, some of it frozen, while the Eskimo must hunt as they move, and they must freeze some of the catch.

Like American campers, but not for the same reasons, the Eskimo need a great many different things if they are to survive comfortably. To make a snow house they need a special knife, shaped something like a cutlass, to cut the snow blocks. Sometimes they also have a special measuring rod to help them find a good place for building where the snow is deep enough so they need only cut out an aisle in the house and have platforms ready-made. For the bed platform they need layers of heavy skins and furs and, if possible, poles and brush to lay underneath, and a deerskin blanket to cover the whole family at night. Then they need a set of short poles to make a frame over the lamp for hanging the pot and for drying clothes. Flint and pyrite are needed to strike a spark to light the fire, and a special moss is needed to make wicks for the lamp. Or, instead, a man can start the fire with a bow drill, the same kind he uses to drill holes but with a different point attached. Then people need bone picks to take the hot meat out of the stew pot and cups and ladles to drink the hot soup. For melting snow or fresh-water ice for drinking—and Eskimo drink a great deal of water—they keep skin buckets on the platform near a lamp. For a window in the house they need either a clear sheet of fresh-water ice or else gut,

dissecting
knife

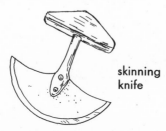

bow drill

skinning
knife

neatly stitched together. In summer, long poles are needed to raise the tent, in which everything is arranged in the same fashion as in the snow house except that people cook out-of-doors, and women and children have to spend long hours collecting brush to burn. Special tools are needed, too: a strong knife to cut up meat (butcher's knives were among the first things Eskimo took over from the whalers), a woman's knife, or *ulu,* for cleaning skins, and wooden and bone scrapers for preparing the skins. Everywhere she goes a woman also carries with her a needle, stored in an ivory case. (The things women first wanted from whalers and traders were steel needles and scissors, precious implements which were sharpened until they became too short to use.) With this she carries a supply of sinew to shred into thread.

All these things are needed just to set up a camp.

But the Eskimo also know how to survive without all their carefully made things, each so nicely adapted to the use for which it is intended. Correctly, sledge runners are made of driftwood shod with ivory, whalebone or the jaw of a whale, tied or riveted to the runners. However, in an emergency, rolled-up skins can be frozen into the right shape for runners, or frozen salmon can be used for the crossbars, or a clumsier sledge can be shaped entirely out of ice. In sudden need of a boat, the skin tent cover can be folded to make a raft to ferry things across a stream.

Wherever the Eskimo are, summer or winter, they must hunt or fish day after day if there is to be food. Most of their hunting methods depend on finding the animals or birds or fish at a time and in a place where a lot of them are together. So they must know the migration routes of the reindeer, when huge herds come streaming across the open lands, moving north or south with the seasons. They need to know the islands where birds come to nest every year. They have to know the inlets where at one season the narwhals swim toward the coast to escape from killer whales. Much of their traveling comes about as they follow the animals on which they depend, especially the ringed seal, which stays in the Arctic all winter. In winter the hunter moves out onto the sea

ice, where it is not too thick for seals to make blowholes for breathing; and there, his harpoon poised, he waits. If he must wait long, he sits very still on a block of snow, his feet on a piece of skin, his harpoon propped at his side, his hands inside his coat, until at last a seal rises in its hole. Later, in the breeding season, hunters and dogs search out the snow tunnels where seals give birth and protect their pups, which at first cannot swim. There, too, the hunters may find polar bears, seal hunting like themselves. The Eskimo also plan their hunting to get the most out of the game. Reindeer are hunted especially in August, when their skin is in good condition and the hair not too thick for winter clothing. The biggest salmon fishing takes place when the fish, fattened in the sea, return upstream toward the lakes to spawn. So the movements of the animals and the continuing need for food give a pattern to Eskimo life, and their religion is centered around this need.

The Eskimo see the universe as dangerous. To survive, people must keep rules which make the world safe for themselves and for others. One of the principal rules, which has to be remembered every day, is that the animals of the land and the animals of the sea must be kept apart. Reindeer meat and seal or walrus meat cannot be eaten on the same day, nor can they be stored together. Women may not begin work on the winter deerskin clothes until

the reindeer hunting season is ended; but all the clothes must be ready by the time the first walrus is caught in the fall, for then all work on new deerskins must come to an immediate stop.

The Eskimo believe that all animals have spirits, and that the offended spirits will cause animals to avoid hunters if people break the rules concerning them. When a seal carcass is brought into a house, women must stop sewing at once, and before the seal can be skinned, the dead animal—or its spirit—must be given a drink of water.

These rules, or taboos, as they are called, keep people always on the alert—always wide awake to what they are hunting, cutting, storing, cooking, eating, or making clothes of. Every minute they must pay as much attention as we do when we are driving in heavy traffic or are piloting a plane. But we think of emergencies—when a hurricane starts floods or wrecks the electric light system, or when a forest fire endangers woods and roads and homes—as interruptions of more quiet times. As the Eskimo see it, everyone has to know every minute where he is and what he is doing.

People in special conditions, like a woman with a new baby, or the members of a settlement where someone has just died, have to keep special taboos. The Eskimo believe that each person has two souls. When a person dies, one of these souls goes on to the next world—a pleasant or a miserable one, depending on how he has died. The other soul stays near the body and is easily offended if its living relatives do not keep the proper rules. If they break the mourning taboos—if anyone in the village dances or sings, if men go hunting with dogs, if women do any work—the soul gets a dark cloud around it, and then it roams the village doing harm until the burdensome cloud is removed. But this same soul also is protective. When the next baby is born it is named after the dead person, whose soul then enters the baby to take care of its young soul, which is still very light and may easily leave again.

Breaking a taboo at any time puts a person in a special condition from which he can remove himself only by publicly confessing what he has done or left undone. A dark cloud is thought to form around a person who has broken a taboo. Although the cloud cannot be seen by most human beings, animals are thought to see it and will then refuse to be hunted or caught. Moreover, this cloud is believed to be catching. If a person does not know he has broken a taboo or else hides the fact that he has done so, other people will catch his condition, just as someone with an infectious disease like typhoid fever can give it to others if he is not isolated and cured. And then not just one person but the whole village may be threatened with disaster.

So, for the Eskimo, being a good man or a good woman means having no secrets that can harm other people. It means keeping all the taboos, and confessing at once if one is broken accidentally. Otherwise accidents, storms, failures in hunting, sickness, and death are likely to follow. When things do go wrong, special people—the angakut—are called in to find out what has happened and who is responsible. These people, who may be men or women, are believed to be filled with light. Each one has a companion spirit, the soul of a bear or a stone or a person. With the help of such spirits, angakut can look into the past and the future, can see the dark clouds around taboo breakers and the dark clouds around the souls of the dead, and can visit distant places and other worlds. By finding out which taboo has been broken and who has broken it, angakut set things right again. But though they can see far away in time and space and can look into people, even angakut cannot see through storm or fog.

You can understand how natural it is for the Eskimo to think of the dark as evil and to believe that evil-doing makes a dark cloud around people. In the short summer months when plants grow suddenly, almost overnight, and it is light the day around, people can travel safely, food is plentiful, and they can live together in tents in big settlements. Their summer clothes are light and comfortable, all the food is cooked in one pot, and there is much busy gaiety. But then in late autumn, in October, after the birds have disappeared and the plants have died away again, as the light is fading there comes a season of very uncertain and stormy weather, when the winds howl and the ice is unsafe and hunting is difficult. Then especially people feel threatened. Later the weather settles into winter. The ice becomes firm. There is enough snow—snow which is now a highway over which sledges can travel, snow which provides strong blocks for the houses, snow which makes a kind of translucent filter for the half light outside the houses. The white snow, the light shining through into the house, the lit lamp which means light and warmth and food, and the bright light on the snow as the sun once more comes over the horizon are all greeted with pleasure. So both the whiteness of the snow in winter and the midnight sun and the multitude of gaily plumaged birds and brightly flowering plants in summer mean life to the Eskimo.

Between the end of summer and the beginning of winter, when the autumn winds blow, a great feast is held for the goddess Sedna, the mistress of the underworld and of the sea animals on which winter life depends.

At this great ceremony, people gather in one of the largest houses of the settlement, where on the floor the angakut make a coil of rope in imitation of the breathing hole of a seal. Two angakut then stand ready, harpoons poised, waiting to spear Sedna as she rises up to the breathing hole, angry and vengeful, lured by a magic song. Suddenly they stab her and force her back, and the watching people see blood staining the harpoon

points. But she is believed still to be lurking near-by, very angry and ready to seize anyone she can.

The next day all the people wear on their hoods strong protective amulets made from a bit of the bird skin out of which their first baby shirts were made. All the men gather in the middle of the settlement and they run, jumping and shrieking, following the course of the sun around the village and visiting every house. The women are expecting them, and at each door the men are given little presents—like Halloween visitors in America.

Then the crowd divides into two groups. On one side are those who were born in winter, who call themselves ptarmigans. On the other side are those born in summer, the ducks. Both are named after their birdskin amulets. A large sealskin rope is stretched between them for a strenuous tug of war. If the ducks hold fast, this is thought to be a sign that good winter weather can be expected.

Next, two giant figures appear, their faces concealed by sealskin masks. Their bodies are stuffed out to a great size, and on their backs they carry blown-up sealskins. In their hands are spears. As the figures come silently forward the crowd shouts. The men attack the giant figures in a mock battle, pretending to spear and cut and stab them until their sealskin bags are broken and the masked figures fall to the ground. But they are revived by giving them cups of water, just as people also give water to the seals they have hunted and killed. Then each man may ask them questions about the future and about his luck at hunting. As the answers are given in murmurs, every man can decide for himself what has been said.

To the Eskimo, any strength may be either good or bad, depending on how it is used. Sedna, whose feast is celebrated in the autumn, can give or withhold the animals of the sea. The angakut, who generally use their powers to help and protect people and to force Sedna to be helpful, are also feared because they may use their powers in a hostile way by preventing the bow drill from making fire, or by killing with a glance. People strive to be strong, and strengthen those who are weak by giving them amulets to wear. The baby's light soul is strengthened by the strong, experienced soul which comes into its body with its name. Babies are carried and nursed inside the mother's clothes. But they also learn to stand sudden cold; sometimes at a temperature many degrees below zero they are hastily yanked out, for they do not wear diapers.

Living in this way they become such strong and active people that sitting all day, dead still, waiting for a seal to come to a blowhole is very hard to do. The hunter has to tie a leather thong around his legs to keep them from moving. When storms prevent the men from hunting, everyone sits motionless in the snow house as one lamp after another gives out and the last food is eaten up. Even then, in the dark, people are not entirely still, but hum softly together until at last the boldest of the hunters goes out to try his luck—pitting his strength against the storm as he waits for a seal so that the lights may be lit again and the pots hung over the bright lamps.

Strong men, who are good hunters, are the leaders, but also— if they are bad-tempered and willful—they may become murderers who disrupt a settlement. The strong forces of the outer world represent the danger of famine and death. Against them, man sets his own strength and patience and cheerfulness, his sense of other people.

Although they have traveled far and wide, old people come back to the little bays and points where they were born—to their own people. Each little group of Eskimo have stories which tell about the past and about the nature of the world, stories which are learned by heart but which are a little different from those told in another settlement. Although the Eskimo have no nations and no warfare, although their language is spoken for so many thousands of miles, each little group has a sense of its own identity—a sense of who belongs—as the people of such-and-such a place, which they know best of all. Here is the country where they know every landmark and every wind and can find their way by the direction in which the wind drifts the snow, where they know in just what place to find young seals or wandering polar bears. But they do not own this place to defend it against other people. They own it in the sense of understanding it so well that they can help visitors to hunt safely there and can be welcoming hosts to all who come expecting food and shelter and companionship.

Comparison of a map drawn in 1929 by an Aivilik Eskimo of an island near the northwest boundary of Hudson Bay (top) and a modern map of the same area prepared from an aerial photograph

The Indians of the Plains

WHEN people almost everywhere in the world hear the phrase
"American Indian," or when Americans hear the word "Indian,"
pictures of Plains Indians spring to their minds—pictures of
warriors dressed in skin clothes fringed and ornamented with
bright colors, wearing great feather war bonnets, armed with
lances and bows and arrows, and mounted on galloping horses
as they pursue great herds of buffalo or descend with war whoops
on some hapless settlement. These Indians lived in tepees, tall
skin tents which could be set up or struck at will. Sometimes they
played flutes to salute their sweethearts; more often, as they prepared for war or celebrated a victory they danced, slightly
crouched, keeping time to the monotonous beat of skin-covered
drums. All over the world children have read stories of Plains
Indians.

When we think of these proud, grim feathered warriors, their skin gleaming like copper and every muscle schooled against showing feeling or pain, we picture them as the proud owners of the American Plains who for thousands of years roamed freely until white men destroyed their hunting grounds. But actually the way of life of the Plains Indians was new, just as the life of the first Europeans who came to North America was new. Many Europeans came from the British Isles and from France to make their fortunes in the New World and gradually, as the settlements on the eastern seaboard grew, more and more men moved west into vast unsettled country—woodlands teeming with deer and beaver, open plains where there were herds of millions of buffalo. Beginning in the late seventeenth century the great fur-trading companies—reaching out ever farther westward—brought guns, iron knives, iron tips for arrows and lances, cloth and twist tobacco, beads and blankets and rum to trade with the Indians for furs which could be packed in small sailing ships and sent home to Europe to be sold at great profit. The towns from which Europeans came were old and narrow and confining; the country-side had been farmed for hundreds of years. And even in the New World, in the new settlements the people's lives were bound by confining rules. So for some men it was intoxicating to have a whole continent before them, unknown land where they could rove, travel for hundreds of miles in canoes on new rivers, trade with the Indians, and sometimes marry Indian women.

Meanwhile another group of Europeans, the Spaniards, moved up from Mexico, bringing with them horses, settling Indians, building great churches and ranches, and preparing to build a great state with the Indians as their subjects. In the north, the British and French traders only wanted the Indians to hunt for them, so they gave them muskets and trade goods in return for furs and sometimes captives. But the Spanish in the Southwest wanted the Indians to work for them—to help build their homes, to cultivate the land, and to care for animals. So they trained the Indians to ride and care for horses and sometimes gave them horses in trade. But to keep peace, they made strict rules to prevent Indians from getting any guns.

But where were the Indians who became the Plains Indians of song and story? In 1600 none of them had guns or horses. Some of them lived in the wooded hills of northern Canada, and some in the country of the Saskatchewan River. Some lived in the eastern woodlands, and some south and west of the Great Lakes. Some lived beyond the Rockies. Some lived southeast and some southwest of the Plains. Some were forest hunters who traveled in canoes. Some lived in villages where they planted corn and beans in gardens and went only on short hunting trips—in large parties to hunt buffalo, in little family groups to hunt other animals. And some were wandering nomads, hunters and gatherers of wild foods. Like the Europeans before they moved out into the New World, these Indians lived a restricted life, keeping to the small piece of woods or hills or prairies where they knew the habits of the animals and were sure to find fruits and berries and roots. Just as there was then no United States or Canada, there was as yet no real Plains Indian world.

The older Indian inhabitants of North America, whose original ancestors—like those of the Eskimo—had migrated across Bering Strait, had lived here for perhaps 15,000 or 20,000 years. Great civilizations had been built by the Indians who moved south to Mexico and Yucatan, Colombia, and Peru. But those who we know as Plains Indians were peoples who lived for the most part by hunting in small bands and in very simple villages.

To understand what happened when Indians from north and south, east and west, moved out onto the Plains in a kind of buffalo rush—each tribe trying to find a great open space full of buffalo, where they would be free from interference by other tribes who also wanted to live on the buffalo and yet close enough to them for warfare and raiding—we must see what happened to particular tribes. First we shall look at a tribe from the north, the Blackfoot, who at the time when the first Europeans came west lived on the grasslands and hills of what is today Saskatchewan in southern Canada.

These Blackfoot Indians lived in a country very rich in many kinds of game. They were wanderers who moved in small bands and lived in folding skin tents supported by strong poles. When they traveled, they made a kind of drag from the tent poles, to which they harnessed dogs; when they had to cross a stream, they made a raft out of the tent skin and sticks. Although they did plant a little tobacco, they had no gardens for food. They knew how to preserve the game they hunted by turning it into pemmican—a kind of cold meat-loaf made of dried pounded meat, fat, and wild cherries—which was stored in skin bags. This could be eaten without further cooking, and a good supply made the Blackfoot independent of immediate luck at hunting. A concentrated food, pemmican was not unlike the rations developed for use in lifeboats or during battles in World War II, though perhaps it was tastier. Some anthropologists think the Blackfoot made a little rough pottery, but usually they cooked in skin bags

stretched on sticks above the fire. The language they spoke belongs to the family of languages we call Algonkian, and since many of the Algonkian-speaking tribes lived in the northeast, we think that the Blackfoot may long ago have wandered out to the west.

Their tools and weapons were crude. Their arrow points and knives were slowly and painfully chipped from stone; their hammers were big, roughly grooved stones fastened to handles by thongs made of fresh rawhide. Ladles and spoons and cups they made of buffalo horn, and they made bowls of wood. Their clothes, made of elk or deer or antelope skins, were decorated with designs painted on with colored clay, or with dyed porcupine-quill embroidery. As ornaments they wore such things as bear claws and buffalo or elk teeth.

In those days the Blackfoot hunted the buffalo on foot—by surrounding a herd and driving the animals over a cliff, or by driving them into a great fenced pen, or by stalking them with bows and arrows when the herds were scattered. When French and British traders came into their territory in the Saskatchewan River valley, they tried to persuade the Blackfoot to hunt beaver in the forest, like the Assiniboin and Cree Indians farther east. But they were not interested. Trapping did not fit in with hunting buffalo, and they had plenty of game for their own needs. They were already a people of the open country.

This is about all we know about the early Blackfoot before they began to move, in the eighteenth century, out onto the true Plains and became Plains Indians.

Even though the Blackfoot did not want to become trappers, guns and horses were enormously attractive, and these they got from other Indians. Their first horses—which they called "elk-dogs"—were probably acquired from the Shoshoni, who lived to the southwest and got horses traded and raided up from the

Spanish settlements in what is now the State of New Mexico. Guns they probably first got from the Cree, who traded them from the northern fur traders. And when, some time after 1730, the Blackfoot had both guns and horses, they became for a time unbeatable in war. Then, too, they began to get iron knives and iron heads for their arrows and lances. So equipped with new transportation, new tools, and new weapons, they moved onto the Plains to become part of the great group of Indian tribes, on horseback for the first time, who rode out to try their fortunes in a new way of life—just as American pioneers, equipped with horses and covered wagons, also set out for the great Plains and the far west.

Blackfoot Plains life lasted for less than 140 years—the period between the time when they came onto the true Plains and began their new life of more active hunting and raiding and the time when the herd of buffalo disappeared, killed off by too efficient hunting by the Indians and by Europeans. Within this period of about five or six generations, a whole new way of life developed and disappeared.

In this new life on the Plains the most important thing was to get as many horses and guns as possible. The Blackfoot became horse breeders, but breeding was slow. It was much quicker to steal horses from other tribes. One of the main aims of war-raiding parties was to get more horses and guns so that they could have more raiding parties. Besides, young men who took part in raids could boast publicly of the brave things they did—called counting coup—and could paint the stories of their exploits on their buffalo robes and tepee covers. In this kind of fighting, dashing up to an enemy and capturing his weapons gave a man much more honor than killing an enemy by a shot from afar. Each tribe arranged these war honors in a somewhat different way.

Paul Kane was one of the first painters to use Indians as his subjects.
This painting is called "Blackfoot Chief and Subordinates."

Among the Piegan, one of the three Blackfoot tribes, the order from highest to lowest was as follows:

> stealing a gun
> stealing a lance
> stealing a bow
> taking an enemy's life
> cutting loose a horse tied beside a tepee
> leading a war party
> acting as a scout to locate the enemy camp
> capturing a shield
> capturing a war bonnet
> capturing a sacred pipe
> driving off loose horses

Since the main point was for a man to show his personal daring and bravery, the closer he came to the enemy at the risk of his own life the higher was the honor he could claim.

In some ways these war games were like sport contests between modern nations, for unless everyone took part there would not be any sport. Since stealthy and treacherous attacks were approved of—taking the enemy by surprise was the one real advantage a small war party might have over a whole camp—and since the warriors fought with great fierceness, a great many men were killed. Except when a party set out to revenge an earlier defeat the main object was not to kill the enemy, however, but to win honor and glory and horses for oneself and for one's band. When new horses were captured, they were used within the band to build up each warrior's fame and to establish more firmly the reputation of the leader of the party or of a man who lent horses to younger men who went on the raids. For horses were used not only for hunting and raiding and racing and moving camp but also for gifts, publicly given and publicly announced by a camp crier.

So the same horses not only changed hands many times within

a band and a tribe, but also were captured and recaptured by war parties. In between such attacks, different tribes traded and visited one another's dances and ceremonies, so that, even though officially they might be enemies, they also learned from one another. Then, too, a great many captives were taken in war, and as they lived with their captors and learned to speak their language they explained how they did things in their own tribes. So each new custom spread very fast, even though each tribe did things a little differently and each had its own explanation of why things were done as they were. In this way all the Indians who lived on the Plains came in time to have a very similar way of life.

Besides the Blackfoot, the best known Plains tribes were the Arapaho, the Cheyenne, the Gros Ventre, the Plains Cree and the Plains Ojibwa, the Sarsi and the Kiowa Apache, the Pawnee, the Arikara and the Wichita, the Kiowa, the Mandan, the Hidatsa, the Crow, the Dakota, the Assiniboin, the Iowa, the Oto, the Missouri, the Omaha, the Ponca, the Osage, and the Kansa, the Wind River Shoshoni, the Comanche, and the Ute. Most of these

Indians lived in tepees, stored their possessions in square hide envelopes, and carried their babies strapped on cradle boards. Warriors carried round shields, bows and arrows, iron-tipped lances and, later, muskets. A whole tribe, meeting for the summer buffalo hunt, camped in an east-facing circle; a leader directed activities and police enforced the camp rules, especially the rule that no one could go off and hunt alone. Everywhere in the

Plains, people believed in the power of an individual man's vision of something that he felt was wonderful, and a man would go out by himself in a lonely place to fast and seek his vision. During the vision he would find out something to help him in his life; afterward he would make a little package, which we call a medicine bundle, to remember it. This might have in it a feather from the wing of the bird, or a pebble from the great rock through which he had heard the supernatural speak to him. These packages, which usually contained many different things, were very sacred. Some of them became the property of a whole tribe.

Medicine bundle and its contents

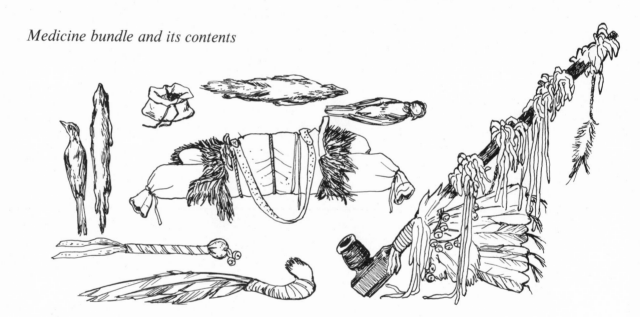

All the Indians who came onto the Plains left behind them some of their old ways, just as the immigrants did when they came from Europe to America. And in this shifting new world, the Plains Indians and later the Americans who moved out onto the prairies and Plains both did the same sort of thing: They very rapidly made up new kinds of societies or, as we would say today, fraternities, sororities, and clubs. One Indian tribe would invent a new club with a name, an initiation ceremony, new songs and dances, and special ways of dressing and behaving; and this would spread rapidly to other near-by tribes, just as new clubs spread among Americans. All the tribes had men's societies. In some tribes boys would join a society as a group and then go up through higher and higher-ranking ones together until they were old men; in other tribes the societies were not ranked and young men were invited to join them as individuals. On special occasions, one of the societies would act as police.

Life on the Plains was very uncertain. Everyone constantly moved around. In the raids and counter-raids people were killed and captured, and many people died in epidemics that started through contacts with Europeans. In one tribe it was said that boys should be treated better than girls because they would die so much sooner; in fact, at one time among the Blackfoot there were twice as many women as men.

The people whom we call the Blackfoot were actually three tribes—the Siksika; the Kainah, or Blood; and the Piegan—all of whom spoke one language and did not raid one another, though they did not meet in a single camp circle. Each tribe was also divided into bands with such names as Many Medicines, Black Elks, Liars, Biters, Sharp Whiskers, and Early Finished Eating. In each band one—and often more than one—important man acted as leader; important men, sitting together, decided the affairs of the band. The man informally recognized by all of these leaders as the best among them became the tribal chief, but he acted for the tribe only when all the bands met together for the summer buffalo hunt and the great ceremony we know as the sun dance. It is not really correct to call these leaders "chiefs," because their position depended only on their actions. A man who was openhanded—who gave feasts, took care of the poor, and lent horses to young men—and who had war fame became important and so also a leader.

Boys grew up in the bands in which many of them would live all their lives. When they were not herding the horses, groups of little boys played together at hunting and raiding—acting out the famous battles warriors told about in their boasts, and testing each other's bravery, endurance, and skill. Their mothers made them blunt-tipped arrows for their bows and fastened horsehair into their hair for playing at scalping. Older men told the young boys how they must behave to become warriors, and there was a great deal of teasing and threatening as the little boys were told that if they were not able to fight and ride horses, they would turn out to be women instead of warriors. After they had grown up, the men who had been childhood companions still competed with one another, and each man knew what all the others were like. Usually young men brought their wives to live in their fathers' bands; but a young man could, and sometimes did, leave and join another band where he thought he had a better chance. As all the bands met every year in the great camp circle, people knew one another and learned about the famous men in other bands.

Within a band, which might number as few as 150 people living in 20 tepees or as many as 800 living in about 100 tepees, the men were grouped into the clubs, the Blackfoot name for which means all-comrades. These clubs—or military societies as we sometimes call them—were ranked. Through them passed one group of boys after another, the way boys here go through school and college, until they were elderly men. The different all-comrade clubs had such names as Pigeons, Mosquitoes, Braves, and All Crazy Dogs; the name of the club for the oldest men was Bulls. Instead of passing examinations to get into the next higher society, each age group bought its rights—its special costumes and songs and dances and ways of behaving—from the one above it and sold its rights to the one below it. However, though the group moved together, each person in it had to buy and sell his own rights.

Usually the leader of one group bought the place of the leader in the next group, so that the same people were likely to be all-comrade leaders from boyhood to old age. But if the leader of a higher club wanted to, he could sell his place to someone else. And if a leader died or was killed, his comrades would decide who should take his place. So leadership in the clubs sometimes did change, and some people might move ahead faster or slower than others.

Among the Piegan, the first society which boys joined was called Pigeons. Like the clubs for older boys and men, this one had a leader and an assistant leader; and there were six other officers, two called Bear Shirts and four called Yellow Pigeons. Other people attached to the Pigeons were four drummers who played for their dances; four older men who could count war honors to teach them; a woman who was something like a den mother for cub scouts; and four smaller boys, chosen from younger brothers and cousins, who made themselves useful. All the people attached to a group moved up through the clubs with the same group; later, the four youngest could act for men who had become too old or too dignified to do things themselves.

There are several interesting things about these clubs or societies. For one thing, everyone of about the right age could join, and no one could be put out even if the other members did not like him. Here, as throughout Blackfoot society, there was a place for everyone; and each person could make his own way, if not in his own band then in another. Similarly, if a man did not have the kind of religious feeling that made it possible for him to see a vision by fasting in a lonely place, he could buy a medicine bundle from someone else. In fact, these bundles, each with its particular virtues, were continually changing hands. Among the Blackfoot there were so many societies and ceremonies and war parties to start or to join that each individual could have a place to use all his energies without pushing anyone else out.

Just as any man had a chance to be as brave a warrior or as good a hunter or as generous a giver as any other, or as anyone could get religious power to cure the sick (though the power gained in this kind of vision could not be sold but lasted for a lifetime), so, too, each band had a kind of freedom. For though many people might die or be killed off, a small band whose leader was generous and just and helpful could attract good men to it, and its strength would be built up again.

Within each band the older leaders kept order. When two men quarreled, the leaders went to each of them to reason with him and get him to cool off. And when a man killed someone, the leaders reasoned with the families concerned, trying to get the family of the killer to give and the family of the dead man to accept a payment. In killings between two bands, the leaders of both would try to arrange a settlement and all the members of the murderer's band, not just his own family, would be asked to help in making a payment. But if the leaders failed, the injured band would march out and there was likely to be a fight. Afterward the band which had killed the greatest number would move away to a distant part of the country for a year or more, and when the tribal camp circle was formed, this band would camp within sight but far to one side.

The sun dance was the great ceremony which brought all the people together, usually just after the summer buffalo hunt. Even in this dance, which brought thousands of Indians together, each part was taken by an individual who had bought the right to it that particular year. The person who started the dance was a woman of great virtue who had promised—in a time of sickness or danger—to do so. She bought the sun-dance bundle from the woman who had started the dance the year before, and the next year she sold it to someone else. The right to direct the dance itself had to be bought by a man who controlled the weather. In the same way, each step of the ceremony—the setting up of the center pole on which famous warriors counted coup, the cutting of thongs to bind the poles of the sun-dance lodge, the cutting of holes in the buffalo hides, and all the other parts of the ceremony —was done by individuals who, usually because of a promise, had bought the right for that year. At this dance some men put through their flesh skewers attached to ropes and danced until the skewers ripped through their skin. The right to offer this torture to obtain blessings from the sun was also bought from those who had done it before. From the smallest privilege to the greatest religious experience carefully preserved in a bundle, rights could be bought, and young men were encouraged to invest in

Blackfoot sun dance

medicine bundles as we would suggest putting money into bonds.

The whole interest of the Blackfoot was centered on life in this world. For the Plains Indians in general a future life had little interest. It was thought to be more or less a continuation of life on this earth, and what was known of it came from the stories of those who had visited the next world and had returned. The Blackfoot believed that a person's shadow was his soul. According to their belief, after death the souls of both those who had led bad lives and those who were enemies turned into ghosts who stayed forever near the place where they died, always trying to do injury to the living. Other souls were believed to go to a bleak, sandy part of the country, where they continued to live in shadow tepees—hunting shadow buffalo and fighting shadow enemies.

Unlike the Blackfoot, the Cheyenne before they came onto the Plains were a village people who lived in earth lodges, houses which were partly underground and covered over with earth. They had gardens on which they depended for a large part of their food, and the men moved out on foot in small hunting parties to find game. The earliest home of the Cheyenne that we know about before 1700 was in what is today the State of Minnesota. But slowly during the next hundred years, partly because they were being pushed by other Indians, they moved west and south toward the Plains—one village moving and then perhaps another moving ahead of it, their way of life changing gradually as they went and as they began to hunt buffalo. By 1800 the Cheyenne had left behind villages on the Missouri River, and reaching the Black Hills in South Dakota, they left behind also their settled life. They gave up their regular gardens (though women still planted corn when they could), gave up their pottery for cooking vessels made of hide, and lived only in tepees, like the other Indians around them. Later they told their children how one of their an-

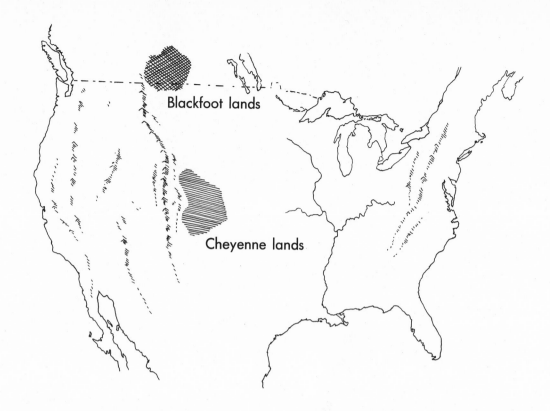

Blackfoot lands

Cheyenne lands

cestors, rolling a leaf into a cone, got the idea of the first tepee! By this time, many years later than the Blackfoot, they also had horses and guns. As they were one of the later tribes to move onto the Plains, they also had a shorter period—little more than seventy years—as real Plains Indians before the buffalo disappeared.

Unlike a young Blackfoot man who lived in his father's band unless he chose to go to another and took his wife with him, a young Cheyenne man went to live with his wife's band. Unlike Blackfoot boys who grew up knowing who was the most clever and who was to be trusted, young Cheyenne men met, like boys who have come from different schools, and had to get to know each other after they were grown up. Among the Blackfoot, little girls stayed at home to learn women's work while the little boys raced and swam and rode and played at being warriors and hunters. But among the Cheyenne, boys and girls together played out the whole life of the adult camp. Mothers made their daughters small tepees, and fathers made their sons bows and arrows, and the children went off in groups to camp for a whole day. Boys played at hunting buffalo and hunted small game which the girls cooked for them. Girls sent the boys off on play war parties and welcomed home the victors. So faithfully did the children act out the details of adult life that stories were told of groups of orphaned children who grew up and rebuilt the whole life of the tribe.

Children were very carefully watched—the girls to be sure that they were industrious and modest, the boys to be sure that they were skilled and brave. Boys had to show their endurance and courage by bathing in icy water in winter and by enduring tortures during religious ceremonies when they ran skewers through their flesh and dragged buffalo skulls behind them. And children received a great deal of advice about how to behave. In telling the story of his life, an old Cheyenne warrior recalled the things taught to him by an uncle, who had said: "I want you to remember that of all the advice I give you the chief thing is to be brave. If you start out with a war party, to attack enemies, do not be afraid. If your friends are about to make a charge on the enemy, still do not be afraid. Watch your friends, and see how they act, and try to do as the others do. Try always to have a good horse, and to be in the front of the fighting. To be brave is what makes a man. If you are lucky, and count a coup, or kill an enemy, people will look on you as a man. Do not fear anything. To be killed in battle is no disgrace. When you fight, try to kill. Ride up close to your enemy. Do not think that he is going to kill you; think that you are going to kill him. As you charge, you must be saying to yourself all the time, 'I will be brave; I will not fear anything.'

"In your life in the camp remember this too; you must always be truthful and honest with all your people. Never say anything that is not true; never tell a lie, even for a joke—to make people laugh. When you are in the company of older people, listen to what they say, and try to remember; thus you will learn. Do not say very much; it is just as well to let other people talk while you listen. If you have a friend, cling close to him; and if need be, give your life for him. Think always of your friend before you think of yourself."*

Unlike the Blackfoot, the Cheyenne had real chiefs who sat in a council of forty-four and served the whole tribe. Every ten years, the council was renewed and then each chief could choose his successor but could not succeed himself; he might, however, be chosen to take the place of a different man. Although the Cheyenne, like all Plains Indians, regarded warfare as the proper activity for a brave man, they chose as their chiefs men who were grave and quiet, highly controlled and not given to anger. When a man became chief he could no longer go to war, nor could he

---

* From George B. Grinnell's *When Buffalo Ran,* Yale University Press, New Haven, 1920, pp. 38–39. By permission of the publishers.

be an officer in any of the military societies. Chiefs served as peacemakers and cared for the widowed, the orphaned, the old, and the poor. So great was their responsibility that a man would sometimes refuse to become a chief.

The council of the chiefs was responsible for keeping order with the help of the military societies. When two men quarreled, both of them were summoned before the council to state their case. When a man accidentally killed someone, the council arranged for a payment to be made to the relatives of the dead man. But if a man had killed someone intentionally, he had to flee the camp and live for many months as an outlaw. If the chiefs could persuade the relatives of his victim to accept some payment, the murderer could return; even then he lived as an outcast who could not share his spoon or dish with anyone nor eat from theirs; nor could he smoke the pipe as it passed from hand to hand. No woman would marry him; if he was already married, his wife and children shared his disgrace.

The contrast between the need for order and peace within the tribe and the need for extreme bravery in facing the enemy was all the greater because the Cheyenne regarded warfare mainly as a test of character. Like other Plains Indians, the Cheyenne continually gave horses away to honor others and to show their generosity; so they were always in need of more horses. But they separated horse stealing from warfare and had special raids the point of which was not to prove bravery but to get horses. So in warfare they could concentrate on showing bravery.

When a boy was twelve or fourteen, he would go out on his first real buffalo hunt, but there was no rule about how old he had to be to hunt or to join a war party. Even a boy of ten or eleven could volunteer, but then the older men would keep him with them so that no one would tease or frighten him. However, when the moment came for fighting, he was given every chance to show his courage. Some boys decided that they did not want to be warriors at all; they were allowed to wear women's clothes and to go along with war parties as storytellers to entertain the others during the long evenings in camp. Other men bolstered up their courage by taking vows to be a special kind of Dog Soldier, a warrior who wore a long sash with which he could be pegged down in front of the battle. And there the Dog Soldier had to stay unless as his whole war party retreated one of his companions unpegged him and drove him off with the blows of a short whip. When a man tired of having always to take such risks, he could let it be known that he wished to retire, and another man who wanted to be a Dog Soldier, usually because of a dream, would buy the right from him. So where, among the Blackfoot, people bought visions and privileges and powers from one another, among the Cheyenne a man could buy a right which forced him to be brave.

Cheyenne boys did not join the men's societies in groups; instead, a young man was invited to become a member of a society in which he remained, but from which he could be expelled for unbecoming behavior. Among the Cheyenne where the girls—like the Blackfoot boys—remained in their own band all their lives, it was the girls who had a society in which one could advance from grade to grade. This was a society of porcupine-quill embroiderers. In the lowest section were those who knew how to embroider moccasins; then came the embroiderers of baby cradles; then those who made the stars for ornamenting tepees; then those who embroidered buffalo robes; and finally those who decorated tepee linings and backrests. When a woman decided that she was ready to move from one rank to the next, she would ask a member of that rank to teach her. And when a woman invited the others of her own rank to a meeting, all those of higher rank could also come if they wished. At these meetings women told about the things they had made, just as warriors, at their meetings, counted coup. Men could not come to the women's meetings, but when a girl celebrated the making, say, of her first moccasins or buffalo robe, an important warrior would be invited to the feast to count coup; and if an embroiderer made a mistake, the only person who might pull out the incorrect row of quills was a warrior who had counted coup. So the idea of bravery was woven into the life of both boys and girls, men and women.

*Cheyenne
quillwork*

Both boys and girls had friends to whom they were deeply devoted and for whom they would risk their own lives. Marriage came only after years of courtship during which a boy had shown his love for a girl from afar. If a girl wanted to marry a boy of whom her relatives disapproved, she might even commit suicide in her despair. But a brave man could not kill himself, though a man who had become blind or lame or hopelessly sick could run risks in battle that would end in his death. Husbands and wives took part in ceremonies together and shared in each other's triumphs or disgrace.

The life of the tribe was centered in two great sacred things, the Sacred Arrows and the Sacred Hat. The keepers of these inherited their offices, and their tepees were like churches in which everyone, even the smallest children, had to behave reverently. Whenever there was trouble—when many people died in war or in a famine or an epidemic, or when a man was killed by a member of the tribe—the Arrows had to be renewed, that is, their points had to be fastened with new bindings. For this ceremony, the whole tribe had to gather; anyone who stayed away was forced to come by the soldier police. Two of the Arrows stood for plentiful food and two for victory in war. By renewing them, the life of the people was renewed and they were purified from the effects of disaster. At the same time the Sacred Hat, which presided over shelter and the supply of roots and berries and all the immediate needs of the camp, was also brought out for everyone to see. This ceremony summed up the things which the Cheyenne desired: success in war and on the hunt, food and plenty for everyone, and a long and honorable life or an honorable death in war.

Among the Cheyenne the sun dance, too, was a ceremony of renewal. Given by a man or a woman who had made a promise in time of trouble, those who gave the dance, and all those who had

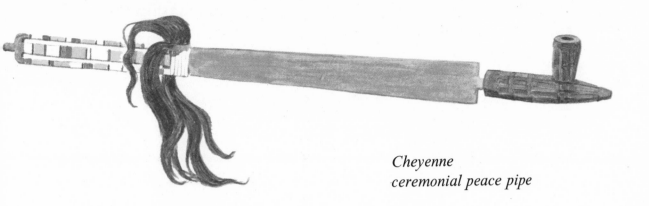

Cheyenne
ceremonial peace pipe

given it before them, were called "reproducers" or "multipliers." By giving the dance, the earth was helped to produce, animals and people were helped to increase, and the life of the tribe was renewed.

Life after death was pictured as a continuation of life on earth. Except for men who had proved to be cowards and those who had killed themselves everyone went to the land of the dead, where they hunted buffalo and lived as they had on earth.

Each of the peoples who lived on the Plains were as alike and as different as these two tribes—the Blackfoot and the Cheyenne. They shared enough of a common way of life so that they understood each other quickly when they met to trade or at a peace-making ceremony or when they became war captives. They also developed a kind of sign language which made it possible for strangers who spoke different languages to understand each other or for a person to leave a message which those who came after him could understand. Each tribe built its whole life around the great herds of buffalo; when there were no more buffalo, that life was over.

Then for awhile Plains life lived on in the memories of old men and women, in the dances still danced by young men who

had never hunted and never gone to war, and at last in the games
of American children who still sing:

> O come let's play at Indians
> Away out in the West,
> I will be the chief because
> I'm bigger than the rest.
>
> Go get your bows and arrows,
> We'll go hunting every day
> With those other Indians
> Just across the way.

The Ashanti of West Africa

NAMES of people and places mean very different things to each of us, depending on the time and circumstances in which we first heard of them, whether we have ever been to the places, and who we are ourselves. For Americans, Africa has for many reasons always been the Dark Continent. But for two thousand years the interior of West Africa meant gold to the peoples of the Mediterranean; later, to Europeans it meant gold which came north across the Sahara Desert in trade. And when, at the end of the fifteenth century, Europeans first sailed down the west coast of Africa, rounded the curve of the great bulge, and landed on the coast, they were in search of the people from whom the gold came. One of the places where they landed, a narrow lowland edging the deep tropical forest, became known as the Gold Coast.

The Portuguese, who were the first to come, were followed by the Dutch and the Danes, the British and the French and the

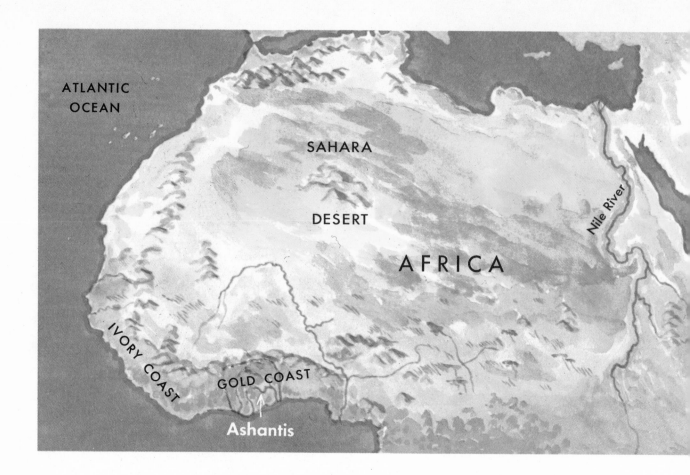

ATLANTIC OCEAN

SAHARA

DESERT

AFRICA

Nile River

IVORY COAST

GOLD COAST

Ashantis

Germans. The Europeans had to land from ships in motion, always in danger, outside the reefs on the harborless coast. They had great difficulty in establishing a foothold—in building trading forts in which to live and in working out relations with the peoples of the coast. Almost everything they needed had to be sent to them on slow sailing ships. Through trade, the Africans were soon armed with the same muskets, and even cannons, on which Europeans depended for defense against them. There were no medicines to protect the Europeans against unfamiliar tropical diseases.

The Africans had all the advantages. They were firmly established in their own country where they knew every tree and animal, every place where a river could be forded, and they were used to the local diseases. The forest, through which African traders and messengers moved in safety as they came and went to the coast, seemed an impenetrable barrier to Europeans. So for another three hundred years the forest tribes kept power in West Africa. By trading with Europeans they got not only guns but many kinds of manufactured goods in return for slaves and gold and ivory and palm oil; and they were able to build up new kingdoms using European weapons, just as the Plains Indians were able to build up a new kind of life when they got muskets and horses.

In African history, there are many accounts of famous Negro kingdoms in the Sudan, the grasslands south of the desert. One of these, which flourished in the ninth century, was called Ghana. The name of this ancient Mandingo kingdom, which fell in the eleventh century in wars over religion and the gold trade, has now been taken by the new African country of Ghana, which became a member of the British Commonwealth of Nations, like New Zealand and the Union of South Africa, in 1957. When the first Ghana was a great kingdom, the peoples who lived farther south, across the Niger River in the tropical forests, were known through what was called "silent trade." Traders would leave

heaps of salt and trade goods which had been carried there in caravans across the desert, and retire to a safe distance, in those days just a little more than an arrow shot or a spear throw away. Then traders from the dark forest would put down little piles of gold dust in exchange. Tales of this trade in gold spread everywhere as did tales of the mysterious people, known as the Wangara, who produced the gold; but no one knew who they were. It was not until Europeans began their exploration and trading on the West African coast that anything was known in Europe about the inhabitants of the dense interior jungles.

One of the best known of the forest peoples of West Africa, a people who are now part of the new nation of Ghana, are the Ashanti. This people, who set out on a career of conquest in the seventeenth century, succeeded first in gaining control over a

large number of neighboring tribes who spoke related languages and then, in the nineteenth century, stood up to the British through eight campaigns until they were finally subdued in 1900.

The Ashanti were at first a forest-dwelling people who lived by hunting and gardening, without cattle of any kind, scattered in small groups in the jungle where dense undergrowth closed over paths almost as soon as they were cut. They had simple tools and weapons and depended on trade for iron and cloth and other things they used. Earlier, they had been driven off the savannahs into the forest by people from the north who had got horses from the Arabs. If an explorer or anthropologist had visited the Ashanti then, he could not have predicted that they would become a great warlike people who raided, took captives, sold slaves to the Europeans, and gradually extended their control over some three quarters of a million people. Nor would it have been possible to guess that they would build a capital city like Kumasi. When it was first seen by Europeans in the nineteenth century, Kumasi was four miles in circumference and had broad, clean avenues lined by handsome houses, many two stories in height, and had a king's palace with a hundred or more rooms and courts, sparkling with color and filled with treasures received in trade from the Arabian world north of the forest or from the Europeans at the end of the narrow trails to the coast.

On a festival day in 1817, when a young Englishman arrived there—the first European to make a formal visit to the Asantehene, the Ashanti king—Kumasi presented a noisy rainbow-colored spectacle. Men and women crowded into the city from the villages, chiefs and their councilors from provincial towns, warriors and musicians, Moors from the north; and the immense retinue of the king thronged the streets and the great open market. The sound of

Figures used for measuring gold

The retinue of the Ashanti king in 1817

horns, drums, gongs, rattles, and flutes filled the air. Spreading wide over gilded rams' horns, the eagle plumes of the warriors' caps gleamed. The flowing silk of the men's robes glowed. Great scalloped and fringed umbrellas, broad enough to shelter thirty people, made of scarlet or yellow silk or of leopard skins and crowned with golden ornaments, rose and fell over the heads of the chiefs as slow processions moved through the streets. The king, robed in silk and glittering with jewels, sat in state surrounded by his family and his talking chiefs. And everywhere, on everyone, gold shone bright as the sun. The Ashanti, it was clear, were a powerful and a wealthy people.

But just as at the beginning of the Christian era no Roman who landed in England and saw the ancient Britons could have predicted the greatness of England, so, too, in the sixteenth century no one could have predicted that the Ashanti would build one of the last great kingdoms of West Africa. Studying how a small tribe of gardeners and hunters came to build such a kingdom, we can better understand the conditions and inventions through which a people were able to change from a small unimportant tribe to a warlike nation which devastated and conquered the country of neighboring peoples and took in and used the weapons and goods and crafts of other parts of the world.

What was it the Ashanti had that made it possible for them to do this? First, they shared with many other African peoples the ability to think about the way in which social relations are organized. In every society we know about, relations are organized, just as every language we know about has a grammar. But very often the people who live in the society, or speak the language, are not conscious that there is any system in what they are doing. For example, you probably know quite a lot about grammar, such as what is a word or a clause or a sentence and what is the difference between a noun and a verb. To invent a new language like Esperanto or Interlingua takes a great deal of knowledge about the principles of grammar. And to invent a new society built on relations between members of families, takes a great deal of knowledge about such relationships, far more than most Americans have. For instance, do you know the difference between a second cousin and a first cousin once removed? This is the sort of thing at which West Africans, among them the Ashanti, were very good.

The Ashanti built up their kingdom by linking together people and land, using the same methods for the whole nation as they used within a village. In their system of family relationships the most important group was what we call a lineage, all the people descended through just one sex from a common ancestor a few generations ago. Among the Ashanti this descent was through women. So a lineage was made up of all the children of a female ancestor, the children of her daughters, and the children of their daughters. Or putting it another way, you could say that the members of a *man's* lineage were his brothers and sisters and his sister's children, his mother and her sisters and their children, his mother's brothers (but not their children), his mother's mother and her sisters and their children, and so on. If you use a circle for a woman and a triangle for a man, you can make a diagram and see how it works. Then, because in the United States it is the male line which gives people their family name, you can make the same kind of diagram by putting down all the people among your own immediate ancestors who have the same family name you have.

In each Ashanti village there were several lineages, each of whom had some land in the village, where the members lived near one another; and each lineage also had other land outside the village, where the members cultivated their fields. Each lineage had at its head a man chosen from among its older, wiser men; the oldest woman in the lineage had a strong voice in nominating him, but all the adults—men and women—had to agree on the choice. Acting together, these lineage heads chose a head man for the whole village, who was nominated by an older woman in his own lineage. This man had to be a member of the oldest lineage, the one which, as the Ashanti said, had "come out of the ground" there. The other lineage heads then formed his council of advisers. Crosscutting the village lineages was an association of the young men who, through their leader, had to be heard when the council made any decision.

In Ashanti, when a man walked abroad his little boy walked behind him, carrying his stool so he could sit down whenever he liked. And a man who held office was given a special stool, which functioned as a kind of throne; he also had in his care the special stools of his ancestors who had held office before him. These stools, blackened in mourning, were kept in a special room in his house and were a sign of the continuing relationship between the dead and the living.

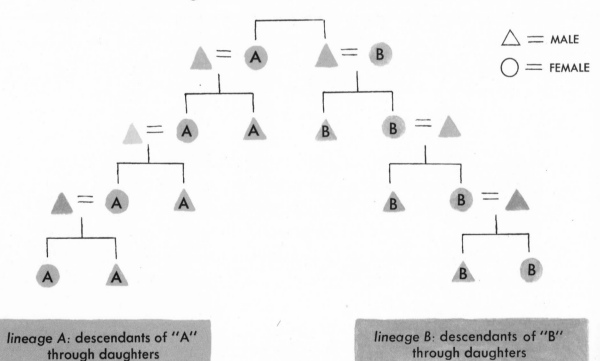

lineage A: descendants of "A" through daughters

lineage B: descendants of "B" through daughters

Matrilineal lineages

For the Ashanti thought of their ancestors as living in a world very much like Ashanti-land and continuing to take a very active interest in the lives of their descendants. The land belonged to the ancestors and was inherited through women, from whom one also received one's blood. A lineage head or any officeholder, for that matter, was thought of as a link between the two worlds. If he did wrong, he could be "destooled" by the very people who had chosen him, because he had offended the ancestors and so had broken trust with both worlds.

This was the system on which the Ashanti built their kingdom. The head man of each village acted as a link with the larger towns, each of which was governed in the same way; and at the top the king himself, who came from the royal lineage in the capital city of Kumasi, was nominated by the queen mother in his lineage and had to be accepted by everyone.

Shortly before 1700 a group of chiefs under the leadership of two very brilliant statesmen—the leader of the Kumasi Ashanti and his chief priest—set themselves free from paying tribute to the Denkera, a neighboring people. And so the Ashanti confederacy was formed, with the chief of Kumasi as the first Ashanti king. At a celebration of this event, the chief priest "brought down from the sky" a golden stool for the king, which contained the soul—the health and wealth and power—of the whole Ashanti people and was so sacred that the king himself could not sit upon it but could only rest his arm on it as he sat on another stool. So organized, with the simple village pattern of relationships repeated on a larger and larger scale, the Ashanti kingdom grew and flourished for almost 200 years.

The other condition necessary for building a kingdom based on conquest and a continual fitting in of newly conquered peoples was trade, a rich trade in which the Ashanti exchanged gold and slaves—captured war prisoners for the most part—for goods, especially the muskets they needed to carry on war. As long as trade prospered and the Ashanti conquered people who were like themselves (but were not so well armed, because the Ashanti kept them from getting guns), the kingdom could expand successfully. But in the nineteenth century everything collapsed. Europeans no longer bought slaves, and European governments tried to stop the slave trade altogether. The coastal peoples conquered by the Ashanti were too different from them to fit into the old pattern. The British soldiers whom they fought were better armed with repeater rifles, while they were still using old-fashioned flintlock guns. In 1874 the British fought their way inland and destroyed Kumasi, and in 1896 the king himself was exiled with his family. But even then the Ashanti kept their sense of nationhood until after a rebellion which broke out in 1900, when a British governor demanded the golden stool to sit upon and it was secretly carried into hiding. In 1901 Ashanti became a crown colony.

Still the golden stool remained a living symbol. In 1920 some road workers almost discovered its hiding place, and after it had been moved, thieves stole most of its golden ornaments. Immediately, wild rumors spread that the British had seized the stool; within hours, the Ashanti went into mourning and again rebellion threatened. This time, however, an anthropologist was working in Ashanti who understood and could explain what was happening. So calm was restored.

So far we have talked about the way in which the lineage provided a model for the organization of the kingdom, and about the importance of a man's relationships—through his mother—to the lineage, the village, the chiefdom, and the kingdom. But fathers were important in Ashanti, too. Men brought their wives to live in a home on their lineage land, and each evening the children carried the meal which their mothers had cooked for their fathers to the house of the lineage head where the men ate together. And, just as the tie to ancestors and land went through their mothers, so their tie to their gods went through their fathers. It was from their fathers that children received their character and their soul, and through their fathers—and all those with whom they were related through males—they took part in religious ceremonies for special gods, each of whom represented a lake or river and presided over a day of the week. Which god one worshiped depended on the day of the week on which one was born, and each person kept his own day as a kind of sabbath. Above and beyond these gods was the Sky God, who had created everything and who gave every person his soul, but who now was so distant that men could not approach and worship him. Earth also was greater than the gods and though, like the Sky God, she was not worshiped, no one worked in the fields on Thursday, her sacred day; and offerings were made to her so that she would help the crops to grow and keep harm away from those who worked the ground.

The lesser gods were regarded as the "children" of the Sky God, sent to earth to help men and be honored by them. The priests of these gods were believed to have been chosen by the gods themselves; a boy or a girl would suddenly begin to act strangely and then an older priest would be called in and would explain that a certain god wanted the person to serve him. Then if other older people decided the candidate was serious and capable, it was necessary to go through a three-year training period in which hard work and strict discipline was expected of the novice before he or she could enter this difficult profession. Fully trained, the priest or priestess served the god and on special occasions was believed to speak with the god's voice, giving people advice when they were in trouble.

In Ashanti there were also medicine men—"doctors" who treated sickness partly by magic, partly with herbs. They too were chosen people—hunters who were believed to have been kidnaped by "little folk" and monsters who lived in the forest and trained by them in the skills they needed. The Ashanti doctor claimed that

he had discovered roots or leaves or plants with spirits stronger
than the disease spirits which harmed people; in fact, he was a
man with considerable knowledge of the natural world.

But it was not only for such special professions that people
received careful training and had to acquire a good deal of knowledge. Every child was brought up strictly—a girl by her mother,
a boy by his father and uncle. And if a man had a special skill,
as a smith or a weaver or in some other craft, his son became his
apprentice and followed after him.

Like so many African peoples, the Ashanti had great respect
for law and order and had elaborate ways of trying court cases
to settle disputes and to punish those who broke laws, though only
the king could order a man to be put to death. The rules and laws
were not written down, for the Ashanti never developed a writing
of their own, but they were on the people's lips in the form

of proverbs. And just as an officeholder could be destooled for wrongdoing, so too any very troublesome member of a family could be expelled from his lineage as a way of protecting the others from being punished by both the living and the dead—the courts or the ancestors. Among other rules, there were many to prevent people from gossiping about one another. This was especially important in a nation where, because many people were descended from war captives who had been enslaved, mentioning other

people's ancestors could be very insulting and was likely to lead
to trouble.

One custom especially showed that the Ashanti thought of
social life as peaceful: when they went to war many of the usual
rules were reversed. Soldiers as they rushed into battle shouted
the insults and blasphemies that otherwise were forbidden, and
the drums and trumpets sounded out insults to the enemy as
battle calls. If the battle went against him, a chief would stand on
the most important blackened stool of his ancestors, to make them
angry and fight harder for him. The Ashanti emphasis on warfare
grew out of special conditions during two centuries when gold and
slaves could be exchanged for guns, and war captives could be
used as warriors, but it was not basic to their everyday way
of life. For in the end as in the beginning, law and order and
respect for the ancestors from whom the land and all things were
held in trust were the principal values of the Ashanti.

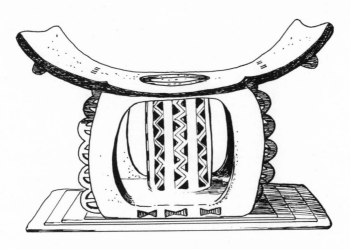

Chief's stool

The Balinese

Off the coast of the island of Java lies the tiny island of Bali, ninety miles long and fifty miles wide, where over a million graceful light-skinned people live. On Bali there is only one day in the year when the air is not filled with the sound of music—the thin piping of flutes, the twanging of jew's-harps, the sound of mallets on bamboo or metal keys, or the heavy boom of great bronze gongs. Most of the problems which were important for the Eskimo or the Plains Indians are absent here. It is never cold, although sometimes in the mist-covered mountains people shiver at dawn before the sun is up. The island is covered with a patchwork of green squares, light in the parts of the island where the irrigated rice fields are being planted, darker where the rice is being harvested, so there is no time when people are really hungry. I spent two years in Bali, in 1936–1938, and this is a picture of their life then, before they became part of the modern state of Indonesia.

The Balinese had highly developed ways of growing food. Instead of an inefficient digging stick or a hoe, they used a plow. On the plains water buffalo pulled the plow, and in the mountains oxen were used. Markets were held at convenient times and places. There people took food to sell and also went to buy food and pots, hand-woven cloth, iron tools, flowers, perfume, spices, and gold leaf for decorating costumes for the theater. For money they used a bronze coin from China, a thin penny with a hole in the center through which a heavy piece of raffia was threaded, so that a string of money looked rather like a thin black sausage. They knew how to weave and how to dye batches of thread in beautiful complicated colors which when woven together formed lovely patterns. Their goldsmiths knew how to work gold and how to set jewels in the handles of their sharp, thin steel daggers, called krises. And they had real writing, although only a few people—learned priests and special clerks in each village—could actually read and write. Books were made of strips of palm leaf, fastened together with string, so that they folded up like Venetian blinds.

They not only had the inventions needed to provide plenty of food and other things for everyday life, but they also had a kind of organization of social life for peace. You will remember that the Plains Indians had made warfare and hunting into such an all-absorbing occupation that when there were no more buffalo and when they no longer could fight, their way of life was over. The Ashanti had built up a great nation by combining agriculture and trade and warfare. In contrast to these other peoples, the Balinese kingdoms were exceedingly peaceful. Each little

Balinese ceremonial knife,
string of money, and dagger

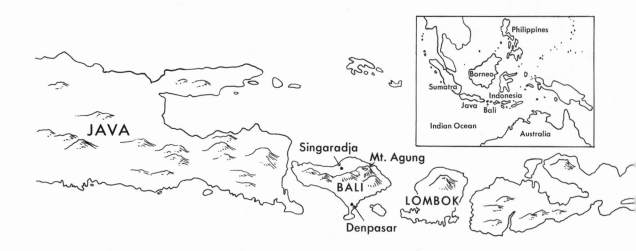

kingdom—there were seven when Europeans first came in contact with them—was ruled over by a rajah, who came from a group of people called the Kesatrya caste, whose duty it was to provide rulers. There was a still higher caste, called Brahmins, from which priests were chosen; there was also a lower caste of people who sometimes ruled over smaller regions where there were no members of the Kesatrya caste. These three castes had come to Bali from Java, and their rule was light. The rest of the people— more than nine tenths of the population—were simply common people. They lived in villages, farmed their rice fields, worshiped in temples, held feasts and festivals, and paid tribute to the courts —sometimes in money, sometimes in things like bamboo or bananas. At the rajahs' courts there were courts of law, too, where very important cases were tried.

Between the little kingdoms there was empty land where no one lived. This prevented the kind of border fighting that might have led to war. For the Balinese knew about war. Many of their villages were surrounded by deep ditches, the remains of moats which people spoke of as "belonging to the time of wars." This is how they explained the usefulness of these moats: "You see, suppose you were angry with someone and went to his house to fight. If you found a fence around his house when you got there, you would go home, wouldn't you?"

Bali came into the modern world only after 1906, when Dutch forces landed in south Bali and conquered the Balinese in one of the strangest battles in history. Dressed in their most beautiful clothes, the rajahs and their wives and courtiers came out in a great procession to meet the Dutch troops and die. Horrified at finding that they were shooting at men and women who did not resist them, the Dutch soldiers stopped firing; the Balinese then turned their jeweled krises against their own breasts. With this battle, the rule of the Balinese rajahs came to an end.

For a very long time there had been a split between Java and Bali which had come about when the Javanese people were converted to the religion of Islam while the people of Bali remained stubbornly Hindu in their religion. After the coming of the Dutch to Bali, relations between the two islands became closer again.

The Dutch built good roads in Bali. They also introduced the system of ruling through governors appointed from the old rajah families. But they made few other changes. Until World War II Bali remained a place where travelers in search of an island paradise could move around freely, delighting in a culture that was very much like European cultures in the Middle Ages except that travel was perfectly safe in Bali.

After the Dutch conquered Bali, people continued to feel that the way to prevent conflict was to put distance between those who disagreed with each other. Children were never allowed to fight even when they were very tiny. When two babies reached out for the same toy, their mothers or little child-nurses separated them at once. When two boys disagreed, they might vow not to speak to each other, perhaps for months. When two families quarreled, they could register their vow not to speak to each other in much the same way that we register the sale of land. If they broke the vow, they would have to make a sacrifice to the gods.

In many other cultures, people may have to spend a great deal of time and effort in preventing boys or young men from being headstrong. Among the Eskimo, boys had to learn not to break the hunting taboos. Among Plains Indians, military societies, acting as police, restrained the impatient young hunters who otherwise might ride into the buffalo herd before everyone was ready to start. Among the Ashanti, every boy was firmly disciplined and held in check by two older men, his father and his uncle.

In Bali, however, the problem was not how to prevent people from being too active but, on the contrary, how to get them to do things—to come to the temple to chop up a pig, or to bring measures of rice for a feast, or to come to a play rehearsal, or to go on a pilgrimage with the whole village to get holy water from a spring. Almost everything in Bali required a group of people to do it, usually a much larger group than was really necessary to get a particular task done. Then no one felt hurried or over-worked or overburdened, and twenty hands did quickly and lightly the work for which only ten were enough.

The way Balinese got people to do these things was by having an endless number of clubs. The whole village was organized as a club, of which each man who was the head of a family was a member. To be a family head a man had to have a wife or else a widowed mother or an unmarried or widowed sister who could do the things women knew how to do for the village festivals. The group of men who used the same water to irrigate their rice fields were a club. There were many kinds of orchestras, and each was organized as a club with perhaps three or four times as many members as there were instruments to play. Each village had many temples, and each temple had its own club. New clubs were continually being formed—clubs of small boys to play jew's-harps, to fight with crickets, or to fly kites; clubs of young men to give special kinds of dance shows, or perhaps to travel all over the island with a little bamboo orchestra and one beautiful girl dancer.

In these clubs the most important person was the secretary-

Balinese boys with jew's-harps

Balinese boys with crickets

treasurer, the person who kept track of who belonged and whose turn it was to do something. He also collected the fines that had to be paid whenever someone failed in his club duties and did not attend a meeting, arrived late, or failed to do something useful while he was there. Since the fines were small, anyone could afford to pay one occasionally. But fines had to be paid at once, for otherwise they doubled and redoubled and very rapidly mounted up to enormous sums. A Balinese could stay away from any meeting of any club to which he belonged, but nearly everybody went most of the time. Club lists were kept in a fixed way so that each person's turn always came around in the same order; a man knew that just after so-and-so had done some special task, his own turn to do it would come. People also were fined for doing nothing. So after a play, for instance, all the members of the club scurried around looking for a mat to roll up or a musical instrument to put away. The fines took the place of scolding and re-

proaches, but because the fines were small, the hurry was gay and playful.

If someone had an idea that he would like to start a new orchestra, or a club to make money by cutting people's rice or to plan cock fights, he announced that he was forming such a club; when two or three people had joined, it was said: "There is a rice-harvesting club that is looking for members." And quite quickly, without anyone doing too much work, a club was formed.

The Balinese had an elaborate calendar with ten kinds of weeks, and they paid a great deal of attention to the way a particular day of one kind of week combined with particular days of other kinds of weeks. We do this sort of thing only with Friday the thirteenth—when the thirteenth day of our month combines with the fifth day of our week—which some people think is an unlucky day. You can understand the Balinese calendar better if you will make a set of ten circles, like wheels for a machine; then on one wheel cut one cog (for the one-day week), and on one wheel cut two cogs (for the two-day week), and on one wheel cut three cogs (for the three-day week), and so on up to a wheel with ten cogs (for the ten-day week). Then if you number the cogs on each wheel and turn the wheels so they mesh together, you can see how the days repeatedly combine. Every 35 days, the same combination of days turns up in the five- and seven-day weeks; this marked the Balinese month. There is an identical combination for the three-, the five-, and the seven-day weeks every 105 days; this marked the first "birthday" celebrated for a new baby. Every 210 days there is a repeat of the same combination from the three-, the five-, the six-, and the seven-day weeks; on this day there was a great feast for which people prepared long in advance.

Balinese calendar

This day, of course, comes at a different time at each repeat, in the sense of our 365-day year, which the Balinese also knew about and used in their planting and harvest festivals. These special kinds of days regulated a great many things—when one could set out on a journey, when one could bury the dead, when one could ask advice or have one's hair cut. Every temple, including the little temples for the ancestors in the corner of every courtyard, had its 210-day birthday to celebrate. There was a birthday for all books and one for all trees. After automobiles came to Bali, every time the speedometer ticked over 10,000 miles, this was treated as a birthday and the car was decorated with flowers and offerings of cakes and patterns cut out of palm leaves. The Balinese also knew about a twelve-month year calculated by moons.

However, Balinese paid very little attention to time in our sense. No one knew exactly how many 210-day periods a child had lived, though his family knew the combination of days on which his birthday came. Balinese saw life as a series of circles that turned and returned. So they believed that three generations after a person had died, he was born again into the same family; people gave to the poor and the unfortunate because they, too, might have bad luck in some future life on earth.

Space also was carefully marked out in complicated patterns. In the center of Bali there is a high mountain where it was believed that the gods lived except when they came down among men on feast days and entered little carved figures in the temples, or the bodies of people who went into trance. The direction toward this mountain is called *kadja,* and the direction away from the mountain and toward the seashore is called *kelod.* In north Bali, *kadja* is south; in south Bali *kadja* is north. So as one moves around the island, one must always find out where *kadja* is. For the Balinese it was most important to know this, for everything higher in rank had to be placed toward *kadja*—the temple for the ancestors, one's head when one lay down to sleep, a husband when he sat down to eat with his wife, the boy of higher caste when a high-caste boy and a low-caste boy lay down on the same bed. Mothers told even small babies to "move *kadja*." If one did not know where *kadja* was, one felt lost, *paling*. This same word also means being drunk, crazy, and in trance.

People had to be very careful about levels, too. Higher-caste people had to sit on a higher seat than low-caste people. It was a great insult to reach over anyone's head. When books were packed they had to be placed on top of clothes. Language also was arranged with reference to the rank of the speakers. Speaking about his own house, a man referred to it as a mere pigsty, but he described other people's houses as palaces. All words—even such words as "here" and "there," or "inside" and "outside"—changed with the rank of the speaker and the person he was speaking to.

Unless a Balinese knew what day it was, where *kadja* was, and what the rank of the people around him was—including whether a person was the eldest, the second-born, the third-born, or the fourth-born child—he felt it was impossible to move or even to talk. So it is not surprising that Balinese felt most contented when they were together with a group of people whom they knew and that they preferred to go on journeys in groups. When the Balinese dancers came to New York in 1952, the little girl dancers liked to sit three in one chair. In their own villages and when they traveled as a club, they moved in a graceful, relaxed, and dreamy way, seeming never to get tired. In their language there was no word for "tired"—only one which meant "too tired." People worked all day in the rice fields; little girls took care of babies; little boys were given a cow or a buffalo to tend. Yet at night they still were ready to practice in the orchestra, gamble at a cockfight, or stand for hours watching a dance or a shadow play.

The Balinese recognized two kinds of learning, learning with the eyes and learning with the hands. From the time a baby could move his hands and before he could walk, he was taught to dance by adults who moved their own hands in imitation of the dance positions—this was learning with the eyes. As they hummed a bit of music adults gently pressed the child's hand into the right position—this was learning with the hands. While fathers played in the orchestra, children who could not yet stand sat on their fathers' laps and learned to handle the mallets. At plays, where the audience surrounded the players on all four sides, children lined the front row. When the play got dull, they fell asleep; when something exciting happened, they woke up again.

One of the favorite forms of entertainment was the shadow play, or puppet show. The puppets were cut out of leather and were beautifully painted, even though in the performance only the dark shadows showed against the screen. The screen itself was a large square of white cotton with a banana stalk at the bottom into which the puppet sticks could be pushed to hold them steady. The puppeteer sat behind the screen. A hanging

lamp cast the shadows on the screen; its slow back-and-forth swing made the shadows flicker as if magically. Although most of the audience sat on the shadow side of the screen, small boys sat behind it where they could watch the puppeteer, for then they were really behind the scenes.

People came to watch every kind of rehearsal in Bali, to enjoy seeing how other people learned. In a village, when a club was practicing a new play or a new dance, a crowd surrounded the players. When an orchestra practiced or performed for a cere-mony, boys who hoped to get their hands on the drum or the cymbals sat two or three deep behind the musicians, waiting for a chance to play. Unlike the West, where very few of the people who listen to and look at performances can play or dance or act, in Bali everyone in the audience was an understudy who watched very critically—more interested in the movements of the hands of the girl or boy who was playing the prince than in the love

story that was being acted out. No one applauded. If people thought the acting or dancing was good, they stood watching for hours until sometimes they fell asleep on their feet. But if they did not like the performance, they laughed jeeringly—a sound which the poor performer dreaded.

One of the best-known Balinese plays told the story of the Witch and the Dragon, a story which, it was said, the people who came to Bali brought with them from an old Hindu kingdom in Java. The Dragon, played by two men, had a mask which usually was called a lion—but might instead be a tiger or a pig—and was known as the Barong. The Barong represented life and was also the patron of the theater. The Witch represented fear and death.

In the play, the Witch, who was angry because the king of the country would not marry her daughter, turned herself and her disciples into dreadful, monstrous creatures who brought plague

on the people. Then the Dragon, accompanied by a group of young men, came out to fight the Witch. She threw down the young men who attacked her, and they fell to the ground in trance. The Dragon revived them and they turned the points of their krises against their own chests until at last they were disarmed and brought to themselves with holy water and incense.

For Balinese of all ages, this play was part of life. Traveling companies went about the countryside with a set of plays to give in villages which were willing to pay for performances. Little boys were given bamboo clappers so they could play at being dragons. Older children formed a Dragon and Witch club, and children drew the Witch and the Dragon. Adults and children and babies in arms watched the play over and over again, seeing how the Witch never conquered and was never finally killed. And watching, they learned that the greatest protection against their fears was to be found in the theater.

Drawing by Balinese boy (age seven) of scene from Witch and Dragon play

The Minoans of Crete

So far we have described the ways of peoples who were known to us while they lived—peoples who were carrying on their seal hunts, their raiding for horses, their wars, and their dances while explorers and artists and anthropologists could study them and report on what they found. But a large part of the most interesting activities of man—most of his older attempts to build strong permanent civilizations—have disappeared from the earth, leaving only crumbling buildings, designs on the rims of broken pots, and plundered tombs to tell the story. The richer the old civilization was in gold and silver and precious stones, the more likely it is that the ruins have been robbed by many generations until often nothing is left to us. We are dependent on accidents, like an earthquake or a volcanic eruption that covered a whole city with lava, to get a full material picture of what an ancient city was like. Pompeii was one of these accidents; Knossos, the capital of the great Minoan civilization of Crete, was another.

187

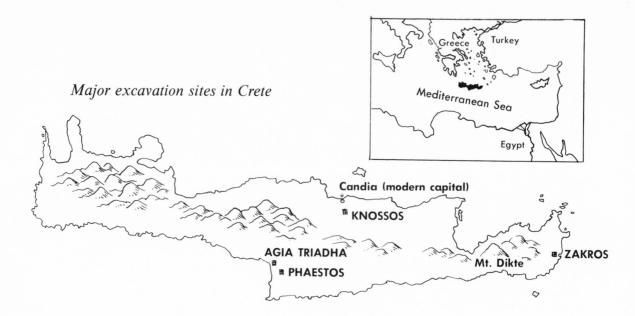

Major excavation sites in Crete

Crete is a small island in the Mediterranean, almost the same distance from Asia, Africa, and Europe, with high mountains which are landmarks for sailors. There for some six thousand years have lived a slight, olive-skinned people, some of whose ancestors perhaps first came into Europe from Anatolia in Asia. In classical times Greeks and then Romans came to Crete. In the ninth century the island fell to the Saracens and became a stronghold of pirates. Later, for four hundred years it belonged to Venice in the period when this Italian city was a center of great seagoing enterprises; and then for two hundred years it was ruled uneasily by the Turks while Christians and Moslems struggled for control until at last, in 1913, the island became part of Greece. On the bare hillsides, once heavily forested, olive trees have grown for thousands of years. But in modern times no one dreamed that underneath a mound here, on top of a hill there, and there, just inland from the beach, lay buried the remains of a great Bronze Age civilization—the first great empire built on sea trade.

True, schoolboys in England and Italy, Germany and France, studied as part of Greek mythology the story of Theseus, the hero who slew the Minotaur and found his way out of the Labyrinth guided by Ariadne's thread. But the classical scholars who wrote the books studied by schoolboys thought these tales were simply myths, fanciful stories made up by the Greeks, not history—just as they thought the Trojan War was not history. The *Iliad* and the *Odyssey* were part of our past because they were great poems, but no one thought that Agamemnon or Odysseus had been real persons, their lives transformed by storytellers and poets.

Then in the nineteenth century something happened in a small town in Germany which changed our knowledge of the history of the world, a kind of thing which might happen in any town to any boy who was really curious and adventurous. A boy named Heinrich Schliemann, the son of a poor minister, listened to a drunkard recite the beautiful epic poems composed by the Greek poet Homer almost three thousand years before. Deeply excited by the poetry and believing the story of the *Iliad* to be true, the boy decided that one day he would go and find the lost city of Troy. As a man, he taught himself Greek and studied the old texts, including a second-century account of a place which tourists at that time were told was the site of Troy. In 1870, when he was forty-eight years old and had become a rich man, Schliemann went to northern Asia Minor, but he would not believe that Troy could really have stood at the traditional site, for there the land was so rocky that Achilles could not have dragged Hector around the walls as the poem describes. So he began his digging in a more likely place. There he found a whole series of cities, one buried beneath the other, and what he confidently believed was the golden treasure of Priam, King of Troy. Interrupted in his digging, he went to Greece and there at Mycenae, in 1876, dug up what he thought must be the tomb of Agamemnon. There also he found clues which might have led him to Crete, but he died before he could follow them up and before he discovered that the tomb at Mycenae could not have been Agamemnon's after all but belonged to an earlier and still unknown culture. Other men carried on the work of excavation. One thing, however, puzzled all those who first worked on this civilization: The Mycenaeans, though they were in every other way an advanced people, seemed to have had no form of writing.

Then in 1892 another clue turned up in the form of a small carved cornelian seal shaped like a bead, supposedly from Sparta, which a traveler sent to the Ashmolean Museum in England. Arthur Evans, an archaeologist, later famous for his work in Crete, who believed that the Mycenaeans must have had writing, realized at once that the carvings on the bead might be some form of picture-writing. As soon as possible he went to Greece where he found other bead-seals, all of which, he soon discovered, came from Crete. In 1894 he went to Crete, and there found even more bead-seals. Cretan country women called them "milk-stones" and wore them around their neck, believing they were magical charms. As he traveled around the island Evans also found innumerable fragments and recognized that here, far older than the classical Greek and Roman ruins, must be an altogether forgotten civilization. And on a little knoll, known as Kephala Hill, about three miles back from the sea and the ancient port, Evans found signs of some huge buried building. There he decided to begin his digging to find out, if he could, who the mysterious people were who had invented the unknown form of writing on the bead-seals.

*Cretan
bead-seals*

The throne room in the palace of Knossos

So a boy and a bead, taken together, showed the way. The work on Kephala Hill began in 1900 and continued until the great palace of Knossos was revealed, some parts of it looking as if they had been abandoned only yesterday. In one room lamps were gathered as if to be filled for the day; in another section of the palace workmen's tools were found where they had been laid down. Here at Knossos Sir Arthur Evans spent the rest of his life, matching his imagination against the broken fragments of pictures on the walls, the work of architects and painters and sculptors and potters, putting together bit by bit the history of Minoan Crete which ended eight hundred years before the flowering of classical Greece and was even older than the civilization of Mycenae.

The great palace of Knossos was not the work of one period, but was built and rebuilt over several hundred years, and beneath it were the remains of even earlier settlements going back perhaps to a period before 3000 B.C. Nor was the last disaster the only one; at least two hundred years before, the palace had been destroyed by an earthquake and had had to be rebuilt. Each time alterations were made some older part of the building was walled in or roofed over; because this happened, archaeologists have been able to work out how one style, one way of doing things, succeeded another in time. Nor was Knossos the only remaining ruin. Gradually, as other men worked, other smaller palaces were unearthed and also roads and whole towns.

As it was last built, the palace at Knossos had many floor levels and broad sweeping stairways. Wooden columns long since decayed, like everything else that was perishable, had supported the inner halls. Light was let in by deep shafts edged with stone gutters down which the rain swept to flush the drains into deep sewers. These shafts let light into the interior rooms. The Minoans had the most elaborate plumbing in the ancient world, unrivaled until modern times. From the palace and the buildings around it, from the paintings on the walls, from miniature figures, from the innumerable seals and tablets used to identify things stored away or counted, it is possible to tell a good deal about the Minoans: how they looked, how they dressed, and what they did. With the help of other excavations on the eastern half of the island it is possible to reconstruct something of their life.

Unlike ancient Egypt or Europe of the Middle Ages, Minoan Crete was not one of the civilizations in which kings and nobles or priests lived in great palaces and built enormous monuments while the rest of the people lived in huts and hovels. In the towns there were many medium-sized houses with terraces and wide windows. The palace itself was built of materials for which no

The great palace of Knossos

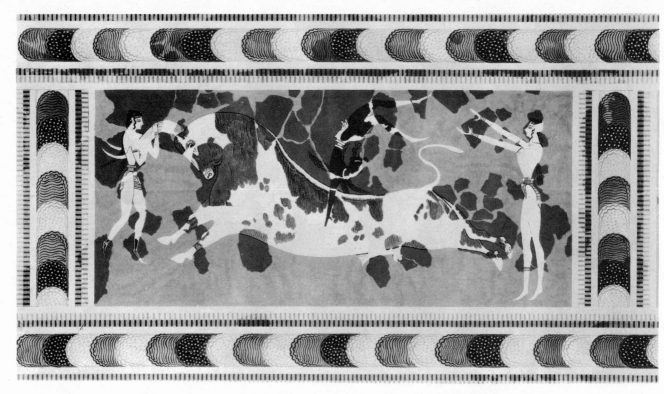

The Minoan "bull-leaping" sport, a fresco in the palace of Knossos

great masses of slave labor were needed. In fact, though there probably were slaves, no slave quarters have been found. As there were no fortifications, the Minoans must have lived at peace with one another, protected from outsiders by the sea and by the galleys —rigged with square sails and rowed with a single bank of oars— in which they carried on their far-flung trade. Women seem to have had a high position, for they appear in pictures of every kind of occasion mingling freely with men. Bull-grappling seems to have been the most exciting sport. In many scenes young unarmed men and girls are shown grasping the great horns of charging bulls and vaulting over their backs—a far more dangerous and exacting sport than modern Spanish bullfighting. Some people now think that perhaps Theseus' Labyrinth was really the palace of Knossos which, dimly remembered in all its complexity and irregularity, must have been as puzzling to visiting foreigners as the Pentagon in Washington was when it was first built, and that the Minotaur was a memory in which the sacred king and the sacred bulls of the arena had become linked together.

Pictures show us young men wearing scanty kilts, broad tight belts that gave them a wasp waist, and leather boots; older men wore cloaks. Women dressed in short jackets and either flounced

Leaping girl

Procession fresco

bell-bottom skirts or full pants with ruffles; they also wore large hats and high-heeled sandals. Warriors are shown with crested bronze helmets but without body armor except at a late date. They are shown carrying spears or rapiers and sometimes daggers, and protecting themselves with tall shields shaped like a figure eight, which gave them room to thrust their swords but also made them vulnerable to sword thrusts. From other records, we know that the Minoans used bows and arrows and that late in their history they began to use horse-drawn chariots. But for the most part, people were carried in open palanquins, a kind of chair with a canopy, if they did not walk on the narrow roads.

There is an openness about many things in Minoan Crete—the great open stairways and doorways of the palace, the unfortified shores, the unarmed acrobats of the bull rings, and the slightly protected warriors. When the great palace fell, it must have been taken in a surprise attack. The conquerors must have invaded the island without warning, killing, looting, and burning—for there are many signs that the palace was destroyed by a great fire. At about the same time, though no one can tell which came first, there must also have been a devastating earthquake. The people else- where in Crete continued their old way of life for around three hundred years. But, though some of the rooms in the palace were made livable again, the palace was never rebuilt and later it was avoided as if it was a haunted place.

The palace builders were not the first inhabitants of Crete. These came much earlier, a Stone Age people who lived in caves and rock shelters in the mountains, little clusters of people widely separated from another, each with a way down to the sea. About these early people we know little as yet, except that they were good potters and made tools of polished stone and knew how to spin thread—for we have found spools and spindle whorls—and carried on some trade across the Aegean Sea. Around 3000 B.C. another wave of immigrants arrived who built towns on the sea- coast. They had much wider trade connections, especially with

Early Minoan pottery

Late Minoan pottery

Shields shaped like the figure eight

Egypt, from which country they brought home new ideas for vases of polished and brilliantly colored stone and designs for seals, delicately carved. These people also worked in copper and gold. So the island flourished and the people became prosperous. On a site where there had been a settlement since Stone Age times, the palace builders began their ambitious work.

The Minoans were businessmen and traders who established posts—perhaps even colonies—as far away as ships could sail to islands and seacoasts to which they carried great jars of olive oil from the island groves, and articles made by their craftsmen and artists. From the coast of Asia Minor to Spain things have been unearthed which came from Minoan Crete or which were influenced by Minoan styles. Indirectly, their trade extended even farther; in faraway Britain, blue Minoan beads have been found and in Crete an amber disk bound in gold, matching another made in Britain. In later Minoan times, Cretan craftsmen crossed to Mycenae, in Greece, where another new civilization was growing and where these skilled craftsmen and artists used old techniques to make new designs showing the life of the Mycenaeans.

The Minoans were also artists who continually drew on ideas from abroad, adapting them to their own styles, and who delighted in nature—landscapes and plants, birds and beasts, and the life of rivers and the sea. People delighted them, too, and there are many pictured scenes of men and women enjoying themselves. But there were also things which did not interest them. There are, for instance, no pictures of historical scenes and few showing

Minoan marine design

fighting. Many activities of daily life and work went unrecorded, and we may never know how Minoans plowed their fields (though we know they used plows), nor how weavers spun and wove (though beautiful, delicate materials are pictured), nor what a family looked like at home.

After Knossos fell, Minoan civilization declined, and not much later a new wave of barbarians swept down across Greece and destroyed the related civilization of Mycenae. Then slowly, during hundreds of years, the very memory of the island kingdom faded until, some people think, it became a legend from which the Greek philosopher Plato took his idea of a lost Atlantis.

The excitement of finding the palace at Knossos was the beginning of work which has occupied archaeologists ever since, as they have tried to date periods in Minoan history by matching styles and objects of known dates in Egypt. So, for instance, in Egyptian tombs there are pictures of Minoans, known to the Egyptians as "Keftians," bringing gifts to the prime ministers of the Pharaohs. And gradually, as new work is done in Asia Minor, on the Aegean islands, in Italy, in Sicily and Sardinia, in the Balearic Islands, and in Spain, as well as in Greece itself, we are discovering in new detail the breadth of the Minoan world.

Painting of Minoan tribute-bearers in an Egyptian tomb

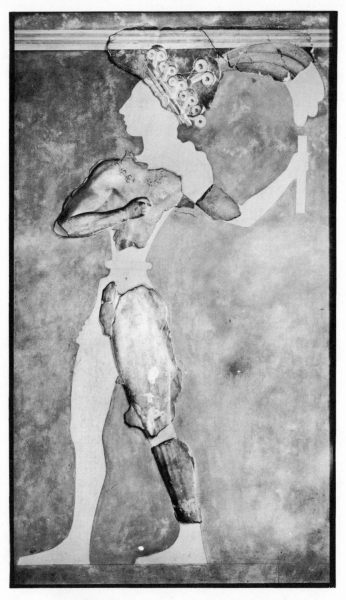

Reproduction of the priest-king mural

By arrangement with the Greek Government, all the rich finds made in Crete must remain there. So the beautiful vases and reconstructed paintings in fresco are still in danger of being destroyed by earthquakes. However, using modern methods, copies have been made and sent elsewhere in the world so these ancient things will not be lost again. And they will be safe as long as the people of the earth do not permit a world war to start in which even the copies might be destroyed.

But what of the bead which took Evans to Crete in the hope that some ancient form of writing might be discovered? In fact, the discoveries which were made went beyond all expectations, for through the writing Minoan Crete was linked up with Mycenae and other parts of the Greek world and also with other parts of the ancient world.

At Knossos, Evans discovered four styles of writing—two forms of picture-writing and two forms of script, which he called Linear A and Linear B—each of which succeeded the other in time except that Linear B was used only at the palace while in the rest of Crete people continued to use Linear A. From these discoveries it appears that while Minoans must have got the *idea*

Two forms of hieroglyphs in Cretan writing

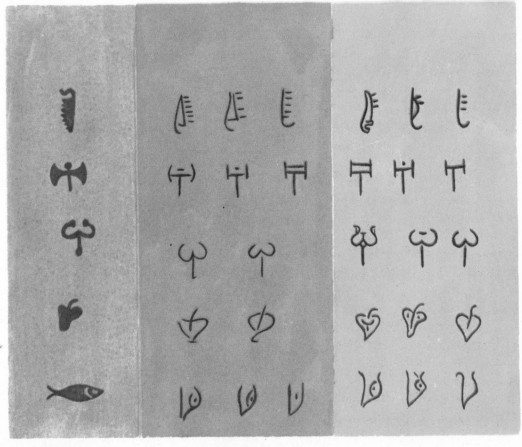

Hieroglyph	Forms found in Linear A	Forms found in Linear B

of writing from elsewhere—probably Egypt, for some of the signs in the early hieroglyphics are like those used in Egypt—they developed their own script independently, first in the form of pictures which stood for objects and ideas and then in the form of signs which stood for clusters of sounds. In Linear B writing, for instance, there are probably eighty-eight different sound symbols.

Almost all the writing we have from Knossos seems to have to do with recording business, keeping accounts, and showing who supervised the work. The earliest writing is on seals or on building stones, perhaps masons' marks showing who the workmen were who built a part of the palace. Later accounts and records are much more diversified, and from these—because often pictures of objects were set down beside written statements about them—we know what crops and animals the Minoans had, what occupations men followed, and what their tools and gear were. We know that they developed an advanced arithmetic, for they had numbers running into the tens of thousands and used both decimals and fractions.

The earlier seals suggest that at that time only a few people may have been able to read and write, for even a man who could not write could imprint something with the correct seal. But later, when the linear writing developed, there must have been many clerks and accountants to keep records on the thousands of thin clay tablets as well as supervisors to check them. We know, too, that the Minoans were careful and systematic, for the clay tablets were neatly filed and labeled—sometimes even indexed along the side—and boxed in special cases and stored away in special rooms on shelves. Indirectly there is some evidence that they may also have had other, more perishable writing materials and that they used pens and ink as well as instruments for incising clay; but nothing of this kind has survived.

But what was the language? At first it was believed that all four types of writing recorded one language, which scholars nearly despaired of working out because they could find no records with translations into some known language. But then, in the late 1930's and again in the 1950's, tablets were discovered at Mycenae with the same writing which Evans had called Linear B at Knossos, bringing Mycenae and Crete together again as at the beginning. At this time a young English scholar, an architect named Michael Ventris, who as a boy had heard Evans describe the Minoan mystery and had determined to solve it if he could, decided that this writing might be an early form of Greek. And he was right. After more than fifty years of work, we can begin to read both Mycenaen records and the latest Minoan ones in Linear B.

With this the mystery is both solved and not solved. For now we know that the earlier forms of writing in Crete were used for a different language. What this was is not yet clear. Some scholars think it may be a form of Akkadian, a Semitic language spoken by people who lived north of the Babylonians. But no one is certain as yet. And when we know what language was recorded in Linear A, we shall still have to solve other mysteries.

What happened at the Palace of Knossos when it was built for the last time? Did Mycenaeans who earlier had been influenced by the Minoans grow strong enough to take over the rule of the palace? And if they did, who were the destroyers of the palace some years later? Perhaps only when the many scholars in many countries, each of whom is working on his own part of the ancient world, can put all the pieces together, will the pieces from Minoan Crete fit into the whole so well that we shall have before us a real picture of a whole civilized world that existed long before the people we know of as our own cultural ancestors began to keep records.

Where Are They Now?

Memory and imagination are important to all human beings. All of us can remember places that we have not seen for several years, and if necessary, we can describe them or draw sketches of them. Old men of eighty years can still recall vividly the first automobiles they saw going down a bumpy road. But besides remembering things that have happened to themselves, human beings can imagine things they have read about and can make pictures in their minds of people and places they have never seen.

Today, photographs and movies and tape recordings bring to us events distant in time and place, in which we took no part. This means that now we can preserve everything except the taste and smell of other times, even the cries of shipwrecked sailors, the startled chirps of newborn chicks, or the wonder of a heart operation when the surgeon starts the heart beating again.

But our ability to make accurate recordings increased only very slowly over time. For Crete we are dependent on man's ability—and willingness—to carve and paint. For the Eskimo, the Plains Indians, and the Ashanti, as these peoples were first seen by Europeans, we are dependent on the ability and willingness of the early explorers to describe in words or to paint or draw what they saw. But for Bali, which came into the modern world only in 1906, we have photographs, moving-picture films, and tape recordings.

This means that we use our imagination differently when we think of an ancient people like the Minoans of Crete and a modern people like the Balinese. Theseus and Ariadne have been sung by poets and pictured by artists, but no one knows what they looked like, if indeed they were real persons or many people whose stories were woven into one myth. But Karba, the little Balinese boy in a mountain village, who was photographed in 1936, lives on—on the covers of books, in films, and in the textbooks which

*Karba
as a baby*

*Karba
as a man*

one generation of students after another study—just as he really was in 1936. And this is strange too, for in the years between, Karba has grown up and married; now he has children who will go to school in modern Indonesia and live a very different life from his own. But this grown-up Karba is not yet known to all the thousands of people who know the little Karba, for this picture, taken in 1953, is the first to be published of Karba as a man.

People like the Eskimo, the Cheyenne, the Blackfoot, and the Ashanti stand midway between the Minoans and the Balinese in the amount of detailed knowledge we have about them. Before the old life of these peoples completely disappeared, cameras were brought in. And so, although we have only paintings of the old Plains chiefs, we have photographs of their descendants wearing Indian dress for one of their ceremonies or for a rodeo. In our imagination, the painted Indians live on, riding over the Plains with war whoops that froze their hearers with fear; but the real Indians are now American citizens, go to school, vote, and serve in the United States Army. So, too, in Ghana the memory of the old Ashanti kingdom lives on in ceremonies in which chiefs appear with their priceless stools, just as on some occasions in England the Queen still rides in a royal coach drawn by eight gray horses. But in everyday life the Queen rides in a car, and the chiefs in Ghana wear modern Western dress.

Though you may finish reading this book without thinking carefully about the pictures you now have in your head for as long as you wish to remember them and without placing the peoples carefully in time and place, you will still have these pictures to daydream or write poems about, to paint, or to use for a pageant or a play. But you will not be like an anthropologist, who must know very exactly just where and when and how and in what order things happened. So it is important to ask about these peoples whose lives we have looked at—the Minoans as they lived three thousand years ago, the Blackfoot and Cheyenne as they lived up to a hundred years ago, the Ashanti and the Eskimo as they lived in the nineteenth century, and the Balinese as they lived at the beginning of the twentieth century: Where are they now?

Cheyenne warrior and horse, painted by George Catlin in the 1830's

Modern Blackfoot Indian dancing group

The far North where the Eskimo live is now divided among Denmark, Canada, the United States, and Russia. During a long period many Eskimo died of the new diseases to which they were exposed and because of the many changes in their lives. But now, with the help of modern medicine they are becoming more numerous, and there are today some 50,000 of them.

But other things have also happened. The most successful European explorers learned to adopt the Eskimo way of life in the Arctic and though the Eskimo got tools and weapons that made their life easier, they remained proud experts in dealing with the difficult Arctic conditions. But today it is different. As newcomers are arriving in larger numbers, it is as if these newcomers were trying to bring their own milder climate to the North. For they bring their own kinds of houses, artifically heated, and clothes that are suitable for life in Copenhagen or Seattle. As the Eskimo are becoming Christians and are depending more on trade than on hunting, they are traveling less widely and are losing many of their old skills. Young men are forgetting older methods of hunting. Children who once wore fur mittens now wear cotton gloves. At the same time, the supply of land and sea animals is greatly reduced. So, although the Eskimo are still trying to adjust themselves to existing conditions as they have done for two thousand years, this has become harder to do. For today they are asked to act as if they lived in the temperate climate which the newcomers keep in their homes and offices and airports. But if the Eskimo are to live even partly by hunting, they must continue to build snow houses, travel by dog sledge, and use harpoons to capture sea animals. Children still need fur boots;

Modern Eskimo schoolgirl

mothers still need fur jackets to protect their babies. Women still need to mend skin clothing with sinew thread. Those who forget how to do these things cannot travel safely in search of food. So families may starve to death in new ways or survive only as dependents on government relief. Today the Eskimo way of life, every detail of which was adapted to the cold North, has been up-set by the arrival of people from the Temperate Zone, who want to keep the Arctic out rather than adapting themselves to it. This means that the Eskimo have a doubly difficult task. For now they must adapt themselves to new customs and a new way of living in the cold.

The Blackfoot and Cheyenne Indians suffered the fate of all the Indians of the Plains. As American settlers pushed west, and as the rivers turned into busy highways and railroads were built across the Plains the herds of buffalo were killed off. As the American settlers wanted more and more land, one after another the Indian tribes were confined to reservations. The worst years on these lands were the early ones, when there seemed to be no future for the Indians. But as time went on, the United States Government set up a Bureau of Indian Affairs, built schools for the children, and tried many kinds of experiments, designed in part to allow each tribe to go on speaking their own language and wearing their distinctive clothes if the people wished to do so, and also in part to help the Indians adopt new forms of living.

The Blackfoot tribes split up. Some modern Blackfoot live under the protection of the Canadian Government and others under the protection of the United States Government. Both governments made many efforts to persuade the Blackfoot to become farmers, marking out land, providing them with farm equipment, and giving them cattle. But during a long and stormy period of fifty years, few Blackfoot tried to work their farms or cared about

*Modern Blackfoot (right) and
Cheyenne children (below)*

stock breeding, and so small was their success that any disaster—
a cold winter, a drought, an epidemic of cattle disease—made
them dependent on government help again. However, they kept
enough of their enterprising spirit so that when the government
once more gave them a start with tribal funds and a tribal herd,
they began to live again, proud and independent. Today Blackfoot children go to school to learn English, but do not forget their
own language. Young American Blackfoot men fought for the
United States in World War II. And out on the ranges, their sheep
and cattle are multiplying.

The Cheyenne have not fared so well. The Tongue River Cheyenne live on a reservation of 445,000 acres of range and forest land

which once was one of their hunting grounds. There they were given plots of land, but few of them took to farming. Instead most of them rent their plots to non-Indians, and they themselves live in one- or two-room log cabins, use kerosene lamps, cook on cast-iron stoves, and manage without running water. Some of them go away to pick beets or to work on ranches. Most of them are poor; in 1950, eighty per cent of the Cheyenne were receiving some kind of government relief. Yet they are not like ordinary very poor people who live miserably in shacks, eat too little, have many diseases, and get too little education—though they live like them. For the Cheyenne keep the living memory of their old way of life.

They still give the sun dance, and they even make up new ceremonies when their young men go away to join the United States Army. They still practice the old forms of generosity, sharing what they have with relatives and other members of the tribe. So no one quite starves, but no one can save for the future. They still plan their lives around events like rodeos, fairs, and roundups; and this does not fit in well with farming. Though Christianity has come to the Cheyenne, they are still struggling to find a way of fitting together their old religious beliefs and Christianity, and both missionaries and the Indian religious leaders complain that the people do not care about religion any more.

Cheyenne children go to school, but educators still do not know how to teach them to read and write well in a language which is not the children's own. Memories of Indian life and the grammar of the Cheyenne language both show through in this description written by a fourteen-year-old boy about a picture he had seen of an Indian woman sitting close beside a girl who holds a bowl in her lap and looks away:

"About more than ten years ago one lady took her little girl out in the woods telling her a story about the fight in the West.

They were fight white man. The little girl was setting on something she got a bowl in her hands, she must be going after something to eat, maybe berries. She is Indian girl, she got a dress make out of buckskin, and the woman got a dress make out of buckskin too. The woman got a long hair and the girl too. That's all."*

Today many tribes are united in the National Congress of American Indians. Tribes which in the past were friends, tribes which once were deadly enemies, and tribes which knew nothing of each other's existence belong to this organization. Among

Members discuss mutual problems at a meeting of the National Congress of American Indians

them are tribes which have almost given up their old ways, others which cling unhappily to the past, and still others—such as the Blackfoot—whose members are sturdily both Indians and American citizens. As they meet they can plan for their children's future—how to give them health and education and a good way of living, the fruits of modern civilization, and how to keep them proud of their past and their identity as American Indians.

---

* From Theron Alexander and Robert Anderson's "Children in a Society under Stress," *Behavioral Science*, Vol. 2 (1957), Number 1, p. 51. By permission of the publishers.

Street in Kumasi (Bowdich)

The Ashanti, who today number almost a million people, are members of the African republic of Ghana, which has become a partner of great countries like Australia and Canada in the British Commonwealth of Nations. Less than a hundred years ago, the Ashanti were still trying to conquer other tribes; in doing so they brought about their own defeat and the exile of their king. Yet in 1924 the king was allowed to return, though only as ruler of Kumasi, and by 1935 the Ashanti again had a real Asantehene. Meanwhile, however, a much wider movement for self-government had got under way in the Gold Coast as a whole.

Young men, Ashanti and others, went to modern schools in Africa and to universities in England and the United States, where they learned to combine their African political skills with knowledge of modern methods of government. In the 1920's an English anthropologist worked to give the British Government greater understanding of the Ashanti and other tribes. Today there are Ghanaian anthropologists, highly trained men such as K. A. Busia, who took his degree at Oxford University.

While the educated young men were planning and working to build a modern state the way of life of the people was changing. Besides the gold which had brought traders to the Gold Coast, diamonds and manganese and bauxite (from which aluminum comes) were found, and men of many tribes left their homes to work in the mines. Nevertheless, most Ashanti are still farmers, but farmers who grow an entirely new crop. For in the last sixty years they have taken over the cultivation of cacao, the Mexican tree from whose seeds cocoa and chocolate come, and today Ghana produces almost a third of the world's supply. This means that if they are to prosper, Ashanti farmers have to pay attention not only to what is going on in their local markets but also to a world market.

In 1957, when Ghana became an independent republic, the nations of the world—including those which once had come to the Gold Coast to trade for gold and slaves—sent representatives

African tribal chiefs gather on the lawn of Parliament Building, Accra, on March 6, 1957, the day the republic of Ghana was born

to stand beside the representative of the Queen of England and the members of the Government of Ghana. Then Ghana became the eighty-first member of the United Nations.

Step by step the people of Ashanti have joined with the peoples around them to take over the responsibilities of a twentieth-century nation. As English is the only language in which all the peoples of Ghana can speak with one another, Ashanti children learn both Ashanti and English. They learn Ashanti so they can talk about the things which are close to them, and English so they can talk about the problems which they share with the other peoples of Africa, with Americans and Japanese and Indonesians and their fellow members of the Commonwealth.

The Balinese also have moved into the modern world. Ever since Bali became part of the Dutch East Indies the island has been open to travel. A few Balinese were educated in Dutch schools to read and write in the language that is now called Indonesian and in Dutch; a very few learned English and German. Village schools also were started for a few children.

As the Dutch ruled through Balinese rajahs, they had very little contact with the villages. The rajahs, who were no longer as rich as they had been, rented their cars to tourists who landed in the north of Bali, drove across the island on the well-built roads, stopped to watch a dance or to buy a few carvings, and then sailed away from the south. There were few visible changes in Balinese life except that the beautiful gold flowers disappeared as people pawned them to pay taxes and that cheap trade goods replaced the old handmade things.

In World War II, Bali really came into the modern world, and Balinese began to share in the hopes of the twentieth century for education, medical care, and political freedom for all peoples. First the Japanese occupied the islands and from them the peoples of Java, Bali, and Sumatra learned a great deal about organ-

Modern Balinese schoolyard

izing themselves into political groups. Then, after the end of the war all the islands that had belonged to the Dutch became Indonesia, a free and independent country. So the people of Bali no longer were citizens of tiny villages but became citizens of a republic of 80 million people who live on 3,000 islands.

In the villages where formerly only two or three men could read and write, all the children go to school. There they not only learn about artificial earth satellites and the United Nations, but they are also taught their old dances. But where, formerly, only two or three little girls would be selected for training, now fifty little girls dance—not to an orchestra, for that would be too expensive, but to a tape recording of the best orchestra. Everywhere people look forward to having their children go on in school, even in the university that they hope will be built in Bali.

People spend less money on old ceremonies, for they need the money to buy bicycles and modern cloth and most of all to send

Modern Balinese farm

their children to school. The water buffalo are not washed so often by their little boy guardians, for the boys are busy in school, but truck drivers now wash their trucks by the pools where once the buffalo were bathed. Better breeds of cattle and new ways of caring for them have been introduced, and today the Balinese herds are renowned in that part of the world.

All this has come about very suddenly in the years since Indonesia became a republic. Nowadays both men and women vote, but the people of one village or one ward in a city vote as a group for one of the parties; voting is not yet a matter of individual choice as it is in the United States or England. Because there were so few trained people and because those who had been educated only expected to become clerks or teachers of village schools or assistants in a hospital, there is a heavy burden on the group of young men who have suddenly risen to positions of great power and responsibility as judges and school superintendents and heads of hospitals. These young leaders are trying both to make their country modern and to preserve the beauty of the art and music which brought travelers from all over the world to enjoy a place where the arts were alive for all the people.

But Bali's greatest problem is one that affects all the peoples of Asia and many other parts of the world. With the introduction of modern medicine, the diseases that formerly killed off almost half the population in epidemics of smallpox and malaria have been brought under control. In 1935 there was still unused land in Bali where people could go to build new villages, and there

*Balinese
cremation tower*

was enough food for everyone. Today the population has doubled, and now food must be imported. There is talk of whole Balinese villages emigrating to Sumatra, and if the people take along their orchestras and temple priests, they wonder whether or not they will still be Balinese when they must live out of sight of the dwelling place of the gods.

Modern Cretan girl

Meanwhile the ancient Cretans rest where they have rested for three thousand years, not one here to help the scholars who are laboring to unravel the puzzle of their script. Until the twentieth century, the Minoan past was as lost to the modern Greek citizens of Crete as it was to the rest of the world, but now they have become the guardians of this past of their own and ours also. And although no voice from that distant time can be raised, the work of archaeologists and scholars of many nations will one day open the records for all to see. Then as the Cretan children learn about the ancient glories of the Minoan civilization they will learn about the whole world of knowledge of the past that once lived in the dreams of German and English schoolboys.

MAN
ASKS
ABOUT
MAN

The Knowledge All Peoples Share

In the last six chapters we looked at five different peoples who lived in different parts of the world: in the cold Arctic, on the wide North American Plains, in the jungle of West Africa, on a tropical island, and on an island in the mild climate of the Mediterranean Sea. We looked at one people who depended on hunting alone for their living, and another who cultivated crops without the help of animals, at one people who depended on horses and another who used plows drawn by animals, and at a people who sailed the seas. We looked at peoples who lived in very small kingdoms, and in an island empire. Yet, different as they are from one another, we still have not touched on the great variety of ways in which men have lived. These five peoples are only examples, chosen to help us think a little more widely about mankind's adventures as generation after generation of men have tried to use all they knew and all they could learn from other peoples to meet their needs—to feed themselves and to save a little store against a bad time, to keep themselves warm and sheltered from rain and cold, to protect themselves against their enemies, and to give their children a view of life and death within which they could grow up, marry, and carry on the life of their people.

If we look only at the Arctic, to which the Eskimo style of life seems to have been such a good answer, we find other peoples living in the icy North who solved the same problems in different ways from the Eskimo. Just south of the Eskimo on the American continent, there were the Cree and the Chippewa Indians, for example, who lived in bark wigwams all the year round, traveled on snowshoes, made their clothes of rabbit skins, and organized themselves around the ownership of hunting territories.

In the European Arctic there are the Lapps, who travel from place to place with herds of domesticated reindeer. These animals provide a store of food and some are trained to pull sledges. The Lapps have much more wood, and they make beautifully carved and decorated wooden objects.

Farther around the Arctic Circle and a little to the south, we find still other peoples with still other ways of living in the cold: hunting peoples who lived in birch-bark tents, nomads who herded horses and lived on the milk of mares, people who lived by hunting or herding reindeer, and peoples who lived entirely by fishing in settled villages on the seacoast. Crossing Bering Strait, we come to the Eskimo of Alaska, some of whom lived more like their Indian neighbors than like the Eskimo of Canada and Greenland.

Some of these peoples lived in places where winter temperatures may be colder than in the High Arctic, and all of them had to solve the problems of cold and snow, but they did so in various ways. The most northern Indians used many of the ideas of North American Indians. The Lapps and some Siberian peoples

Birch-bark tepee in snow

drew on Old World knowledge of domesticated animals. So we can see that the kind of country, the climate and the animals and plants and other materials, limits what a people can do. But it does not determine what they will do. Where there is no snow, it is impossible to build snow houses; but just because there is a great deal of snow, men will not necessarily build snow houses, nor will the knowledge that their neighbors build snow houses necessarily lead a people to give up their skin tents or lodges of wood.

Through the centuries mankind has learned how to solve the basic problems of keeping alive. And although the solutions worked out by one people differ from those of another people, we find that if we include the whole world, there are some things that human beings everywhere in the world know about—the things that are necessary if people are to live together in communities.

The idea of being wrecked on a desert island has always appealed to man's imagination, and most peoples have some story describing what the hero did to stay alive. Such stories bring us face to face with what being human and staying human means. The most famous of these stories is *Robinson Crusoe,* by Daniel Defoe. It was published in 1719 at just the period when English explorers and settlers were writing accounts of how primitive peoples lived. In this same century Captain Cook and other explorers sailed the Pacific and brought home tales of how the islanders lived in what seemed a kind of paradise where no one was ever cold or hungry; and, of course, the colonists in America also brought back stories about the American Indian, the tall proud Redskin. People were being shaken out of their narrow little worlds, and they began to speculate about mankind and the kind of life men had lived in earlier times.

If you have never imagined what it would be like to be wrecked on a desert island with nothing—nothing at all but the shorts and shirt you were wearing—and have never wondered how you would manage to live, you might try imagining it. Probably you would want to have with you at least one companion, or perhaps your whole family or the family of one of your friends with whom you like going on camping trips. After you have picked your companions and have settled on the kind of accident that would leave you stranded, you can start to think out what you would do. Before you read any further in this chapter, you might make a list of things that would have to be taken care of. Then you can match your list of what you know about with what anthropologists have found out by studying peoples all over the world and what they have learned by considering the tools and other archaeological remains of peoples who have long since disappeared from the earth.

At home you live in a world in which you are dependent on

things that happen miles, even continents, away from you. The electricity which lights your house and the gas on which you cook may come from far away, and a storm of which you never feel a breath may cause a break in the power line and leave you without water or light or heat or cold to preserve the food in the deep freeze. Telephone lines may break down, the roads may be flooded, the railroad may go out of service, no planes may land. Suddenly civilized men and women living in houses which have drawn on the inventions of centuries—roofs that do not leak, ceilings, stairs, windows, doors (all of which had to be invented), to say nothing of electric stoves, indoor plumbing, and furnaces governed by thermostats—have to find out how to manage without the equipment to which they are accustomed.

But trying to live in a house when the power has temporarily failed is quite a different thing from trying to live on an island

An American home demolished by a tornado

with nothing to help you but your hands and brains and your own knowledge of what man has done before. During World War II, American fliers faced the danger of having to make emergency landings in the wilds of New Guinea, where they might or might not meet any people. So two kinds of training were given to them: training in what to do if they met some savages who had never seen strangers really different from themselves, and training in what to do if they met no people at all.

The first kind of training was intended to teach the fliers to respect the people they might meet. Of course, they would not be able to talk with them, but as all human beings get hungry and need food, get thirsty and need water, get tired and need rest, these are needs that all human beings can understand; and the idea of what is wanted can easily be put into understandable sign language. Then, as all human beings have some ideas about strangers, the fliers were taught that they would have to convince the natives that they were friendly and needed help, but that they were not so weak and helpless that they could easily be killed, and that, as they were human beings like their hosts, they really could understand each other. (When you come to think of it, these are also the things that the people of a modern nation need to convince other modern nations of: their friendliness, their need for co-operation—by which they do not mean the weakness that tempts others to bully or conquer—and their belief that even though two peoples do not speak the same language or have the same religion, they can understand each other.)

The fliers were warned how differently people communicate with each other. A nod of the head might mean No instead of Yes; a shake of the head might mean Yes; raised eyebrows might mean only a simple question. Being patted all over by the men of the tribe might be a gesture of great friendliness and not, as one might suspect, an attempt to find out if a person was fat enough to be eaten. They had to learn that, lost in a remote mountain valley, the only thing they could really count on was that their respect for other human beings and their trust in them would somehow show in their faces and be heard in their voices, despite all the differences between their hosts and themselves—in skin color and appearance, in the meaning of gestures—and despite the barrier of thousands of years of difference in civilization.

But they also needed training in what to do if there were no natives to help them. New Guinea is a very large island where one can sometimes travel for days without seeing a single human being. Once when I was going up the wide Sepik River on my way to study one of the river peoples, the schooner on which I was traveling ran aground on a hidden sand bank. We tried the usual method of getting off a sand bank, throwing overboard the gasoline tanks attached to ropes. Nothing happened. We could see that it was going to take more human effort than our crew could supply to get us off, but surely canoes of river people would soon come along. None came. The great river, filled with crocodiles, flowed by hour after hour. Finally, late in the day an earthquake shook us free. Otherwise we might have remained there for several days before a canoe came by.

Our World War II fliers had to know how to depend only on themselves and how to protect themselves, how to find food and how to use the unfamiliar plants to make what they needed, and how to mark their course so that they would not wander in a circle. Anthropologists who had spent years studying how Pacific Islanders lived were the teachers in the school for these fliers. They also taught those who might be stranded on an atoll, a low coral island, on which they might find no growing thing except palm trees, how to start a fire by using the glass from a watch and how to get food and drink and fuel and clothes and shelter by using the products of the trees. They even taught them how to fashion a hook and line from coconut fiber and a shell so they could fish.

This school was necessary for two reasons. Modern civilized man has had no practice in living without a whole collection of tools and weapons, and our fliers would not have time to sit down and think and experiment. But now, instead of fliers stranded during wartime, let us think of a group of people from our own or some other society, who have enough food to last for several days but no equipment, and who land in a place where there is an abundance of plants and animals. Then we can ask: *What are the things that all human beings understand are a necessary part of being human and that all human beings, no matter how savage, would try to set up again?*

First would come the question of shelter. Nowhere in the world is there a people who do not know how to build some kind of protection against the weather—wind and rain, heat and cold. But methods of providing shelter vary enormously. We have looked at the snow house and the summer tent of the Eskimo, the earth lodge and the tepee of the Plains Indians, the thatch-roofed clay house of the Ashanti, the Balinese house with walls made of woven bamboo or wood or stone and a roof of thatch

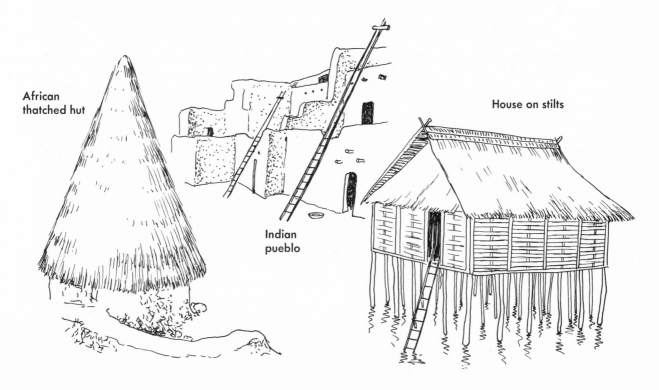

African thatched hut

Indian pueblo

House on stilts

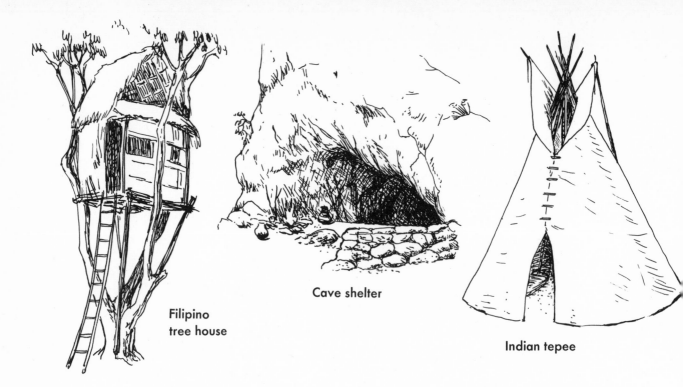

Filipino
tree house

Cave shelter

Indian tepee

or bamboo tiles, and the many-storied, stone-and-wood palace of Knossos. Where there are caves, people have lived in them from time to time. Other peoples have built their houses in trees to be safe from wild animals; or they have perched them on stilts over water to be near their fishing grounds; or they have cut apartments out of a cliff and protected themselves against enemies by pulling up their ladders. The kind of shelter our castaways would try to build would depend on the part of the world and the culture from which they came. But we can be quite sure that they would know about shelter and would have some idea how a roof could be supported and would look for materials to cover the roof.

If you think about the idea of a roof—something we all take for granted—you can see that in its most basic form it is something to keep the rain or snow or heat from what is under it. Of course, if you know a roof is necessary, you can start over again to invent something new. But you would be more likely to think first of the kind of roof you were most familiar with, like the steeply sloping New England roof down which the snow can slide, the flat roof of the Southwest on which people sit at night,

Types of roof forms

or if you had been a camper, you might perhaps think of a tepee or a wigwamlike structure—a big cone coming to a point at the top, which in a sense is all roof.

If you had read about primitive peoples and had visited museums and studied the models of houses you saw there, you would not be limited to making just one kind of roof which might not be practical on your island. For if you think about it, you will realize that special materials are needed for each kind of roof. A tepee is usually made of the skins of animals sewn together; a wigwam is made of birch bark; a tent is made of woven cloth or felt. For a flat roof some kind of beam is needed, the trunk of a tree or slabs of worked stone. An arched roof can be made with bent boughs or with whalebone.

If none of these materials was available, you might perhaps remember how people have made stone roofs using either the method of the corbeled arch or the method of the true arch. In a

Mayan temple, with diagram of corbeled arch

Roman aqueduct, with diagram of true arch

corbeled arch each layer of stones projects a little further toward the center until the two edges meet. In a true arch each stone or brick is slightly wedge-shaped, and all pieces forming the arch are held in place by the keystone at the top. No people in the New World had the idea of the true arch. Many peoples in the world have used the corbeled arch, but in the New World only the Maya of Yucatan worked out the idea. The principle of the keystone was discovered by the ancient Mesopotamians and using it, people could build great vaulted ceilings as in the church of Saint Sophia in Istanbul, in which the great central dome rests on four huge arches, or the soaring pointed arches of Gothic cathedrals, such as Notre Dame in Paris or Saint Patrick's in New York.

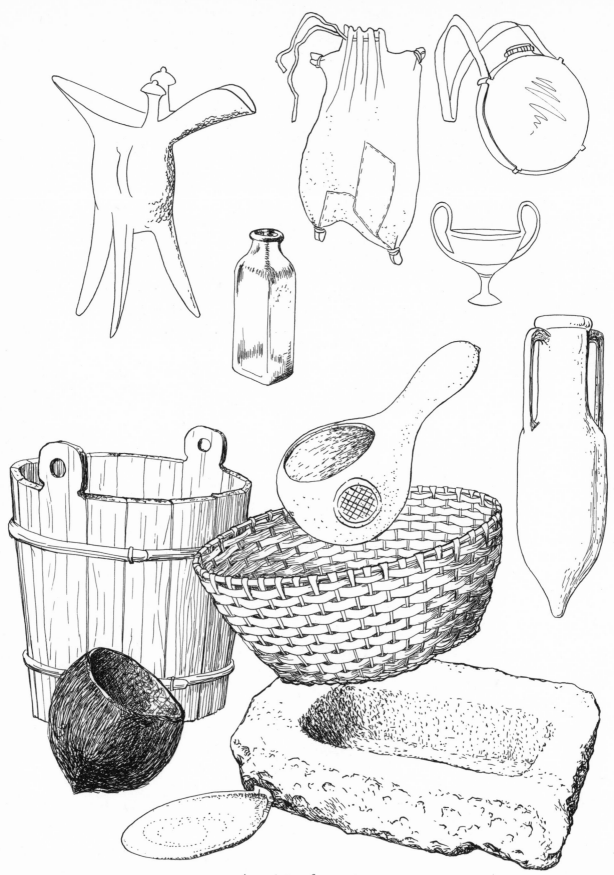

A variety of containers

The more freely our castaways could draw on the history of man, the more they would know about the different materials—wood, stone, bone, horn, shell, leaves, skin, the shells of such fruits as coconuts and gourds—man has used to make containers and tools and weapons. An ape will pick up a stick or a stone to use as a temporary tool, and many living creatures use teeth or bill or claws to fashion shelters in ways peculiar to their species. But man alone has everywhere had the idea of a tool—of making an object which can then be used to work on other objects—to cut down a tree, to cut off bark, to skin an animal, or to polish a stone. Every people have some tools, something to hammer with, something to cut and scrape with.

So also every people have the idea of a weapon if we use this word in the widest sense to mean something with which one can take the life of a living creature, as a fish, a bird, a bear, a man. Most peoples have more complicated ideas than this, for they have some weapons which they use specially for hunting and others for warfare against other human beings, weapons of offense and defense. But nowhere does man depend on his bare hands alone. As tools increase the skill and strength of his hands to make other things, so weapons increase his ability to use the living things of the world and to defend himself against those living things which try to use him or defend themselves against him.

The idea of a tool to make another tool is a very old one. The stone hammer which early man used to chip or flake a piece of flint to the desired shape was such a tool. Today we have computers which can work out designs for other kinds of machines, in which the computer, like the hammer, is used to make another tool of a different sort. Though it is a tremendous leap from the stone hammer to the computer, once the idea of a tool to make another tool was invented, the way was opened for the whole series of inventions that led up to the dissecting tool than can be

Different kinds of tools

used only under a microscope or the modern computer. The way was opened, but for hundreds of generations it was not taken. Our castaways would find themselves back at a very early stage as they looked around for a stone with which to sharpen something—another stone, a piece of wood, a shell to serve them as a knife.

The idea of some kind of weapon which can be used at a safe distance from the quarry is also a very old one. The javelin, the slingshot, the bolas, the spear thrower, the bow and arrow, the blow gun, or the boomerang (that remarkable invention of the

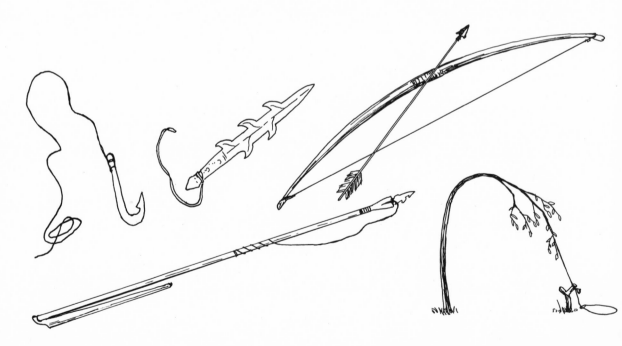

Different kinds of weapons

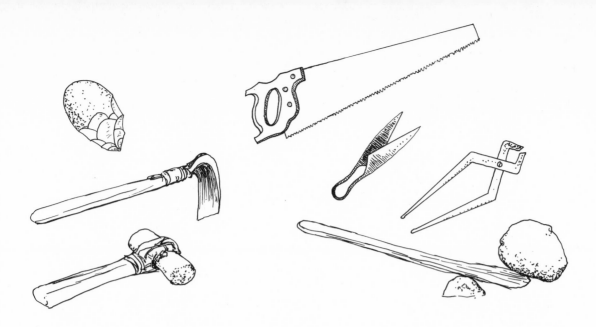

Australian aborigines—a curved piece of wood with a cutting edge which is thrown through the air and returns to the hunter if it fails of its mark) are all primitive ways of killing at a distance. A hook and line enables the fisherman to catch fish in deep water, and a harpoon enables him to kill and haul in a swift and heavy creature. So, too, snares and traps and pitfalls are ways of catching the elusive quarry. Our castaways, looking over their situation and thinking of their need for weapons for hunting and fishing and possibly for defense, would have some idea of a hitting or thrusting weapon, of a weapon that could somehow be sent through

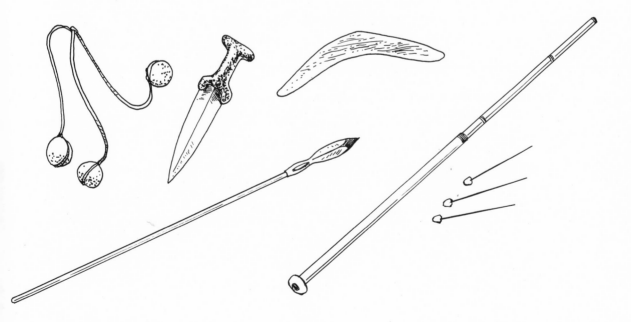

the air or water, and of a trap of some sort into which the unwary bird or beast or fish would come.

They would, of course, know that it is possible for man to support life by eating berries, fruits, seeds, and roots, but they would also know that some of these are edible while others are not. If they were stranded on an island where all the plants and trees were strange to them, this knowledge would be more frightening than helpful, for they would realize that any one of the tempting fruits that hung lush on the trees might be poisonous, and they would have none of the knowledge that each people pass down from one generation to the next about what can be eaten with safety. Their own knowledge of safe foods had in this way come down to them from a time when people died accidentally and someone made the necessary observation that eating this berry or that root resulted in death. And since not all peoples have domesticated animals, they might have no idea of how to find out whether a particular food was poisonous or not. In this perhaps more than in anything else, they would realize how helpless man is without a precise knowledge of the living world around him and how precious this inheritance is.

If someone was injured or became sick, the castaways would also be faced with the problem of how to care for him—how to stop the bleeding or straighten the bone, or how to find a remedy for the fever or the pain. About this, all we can be certain of is that any group of human beings would have some idea of trying to do something. If in the past they had depended on special leaves or plants, they would have to search for substitutes, but as they would have no way of knowing as a botanist would whether the plants they found worked in any way like the ones they had known before, they would not have very much to rely on. Every people in the world have some way of asking for or commanding help from supernaturals. If they had brought with them magic charms, or had the idea of praying or of making offerings to some spirit, they would try this.

If the climate was cold, the question of some kind of clothing would come up sooner or later. None of the ways in which clothes have been made is shared by all peoples. Some peoples know how to plait or weave mats which are so fine that they can be used as cloth. Some peoples know how to tailor clothes from skins. Some have looms and know how to weave cloth. Other peoples fray leaves into thick fringes out of which they make skirts or kilts. Still other peoples know how to beat the inner bark of certain trees into a thin substance like paper facial tissues, sheets of which they paste together to make bark cloth. But none of these inventions is world-wide, so we can only be sure that our castaways would start off with the knowledge that leaves and bark and reeds could be used, and perhaps if they were meeting cold for the first time, they might survive if it was not too cold.

Types of clothing

But whether they would survive in a cold climate would also depend on whether they knew how to make fire. Most peoples know how to make fire; some few peoples only know how to keep it, carefully guarding the flame which they got from a log struck by lightning or perhaps from another people, all of whom they killed before they learned what the secret was. Archaeologists think that the keeping of fire is much older than the making of it, and this may explain why there are in different parts of the world so many ways of starting a fire—with the fire plow, the fire drill, the fire bow, flint and pyrite, and so on. So while we could be sure that our castaways would know about the use of fire, they might not know how to make it, though the chances are high that they would.

Everything we have discussed so far has been concerned with using things—sticks and stones and leaves and shells for tools and weapons, shelter and clothing; berries and fruit and roots, fish and shellfish and birds and small animals for food. But while they were exploring their surroundings and testing out materials, our castaways would also need to arrange some kind of formal relationships among themselves.

Arranging space is one way of arranging people, and one thing all human groups know about is arranging space in some way so that each person has a place in it. We have seen how complicated this can be. The Eskimo snow hut had built into it

Typical small house, U. S. A.

a place for each woman's fire, places for storing food and equipment, and a place in the passage for the dogs to shelter themselves during a storm. In a Plains Indian tepee, there was a man's part and a woman's part and a place for the sacred medicine bundles. In Bali every act was related to direction—to the center of the island. So, too, if you look at an American town, you will see that people live and work and play in different places; and in American homes there are separate rooms or areas for eating and sleeping and entertaining, for preparing food and washing clothes. Through all these different arrangements runs the idea that it is necessary for a group of people to arrange themselves and their possessions in space.

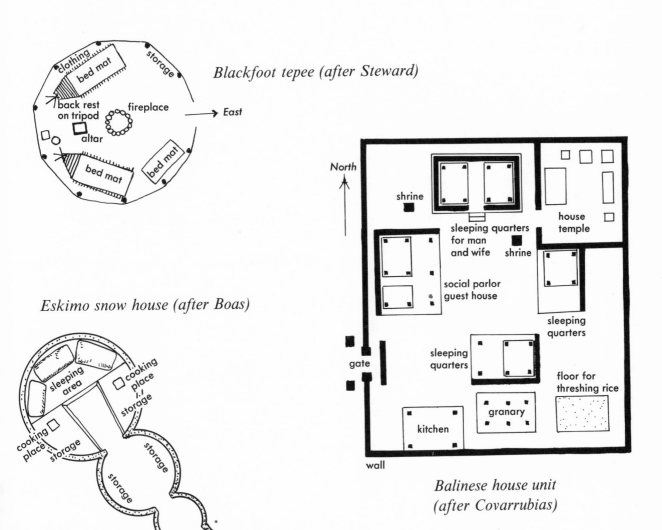

Blackfoot tepee (after Steward)

Eskimo snow house (after Boas)

Balinese house unit (after Covarrubias)

Whatever shelter our castaways found or built for themselves, they would make some arrangement so that each person would have some space for himself, and as soon as there were families, so that each family would have a shelter or part of a shelter for itself. Though this might be no more than a place to spread a mat for a bed and a bent branch to hang things on, it would belong to one family and no other.

With the arrangement of space would go rules about property and privacy: rules about the conditions under which people could enter the bit of space that belonged to someone else and about when taking something belonging to another person was all right and when it was not all right and was considered stealing. You will remember that the Eskimo had quite different ideas from ours about property. For instance, a man would lend his wife to another man, and when people took soapstone from a rock, they would leave a "present" for the rock. There are peoples who treat the individual's name as such private property that no one may ever speak it aloud. And some peoples have houses which no one except the owners may ever enter. Yet the only thing we can be certain of is that our castaways would have ideas about property and privacy which were made clear by positions in space, for these are universal human ideas.

Whether people could keep up their old ideas of space and privacy would depend on whether these old ideas had been very closely tied in with the way the house was built or with the shape and position of the fireplace. In the snow house, the Eskimo woman's soapstone lamp with its drying rack and cooking pot showed which side of the house was hers, but even in summer when people lived in tents and cooked out-of-doors the division of the house remained the same. In the Plains, the places where things were kept were related to the conical shape of the tepee.

On a strange island, where people built a new kind of house using new kinds of materials, many of the old ways would disappear—the particular ways by which they had made clear who was host and who was guest in a house and what sacred objects a man kept there. But the ideas themselves would be there just the same.

They would know, too, that it is necessary to have rules about how a family is organized, including rules about when children may marry, rules to keep fathers from marrying their daughters, or mothers from marrying their sons, or brothers from marrying their sisters, and rules about which men should take care of the mothers of young children. Though in most human societies a woman's husband helps to bring up her children, in some a man helps his sister, and in others the main responsibility falls on one of the two grandfathers. People everywhere recognize that children need to be cared for by persons of both sexes and know that the way to organize the world is to have rules defining who the persons are who take care of a child.

But some of the familiar rules might not be workable. Though in the past strong men might have had several wives, this could not be done if there were no extra women among the group of castaways. However, if there were men and women old enough to marry, they could be paired off; people everywhere in the world have the idea of the married couple. In this case the old abandoned form of marriage, in which a man had several wives or a woman had several husbands, might survive in memory or it might not.

Women would breastfeed their babies, for this is something human beings anywhere can do. The idea of giving babies cow or goat's milk or of making artificial foods for them is a recent one which is not known in many parts of the world. Some peoples do not have the idea that if a mother takes sick or dies, another woman who has milk can feed the baby. Even this very simple idea is a cultural invention.

So although we cannot say what the rules would be, we can be sure that our castaways would know that there need to be rules for marriage, for taking care of children, for sorting out people, and for deciding who belonged with whom and who was responsible for whom.

Of course, these people would have a language, for all human beings have languages; and all languages, however different from one another, can be used to express any idea which anyone may have even though if the idea is an unfamiliar one, it may take a great many words to do so. But we cannot be sure that the castaways would have any form of writing or of keeping records or any way of sending messages. Even such a crude and simple thing as the Plains Indian winter count is unknown to some of the peoples of the world.

Nor could we expect that they would necessarily know very much about time. They would certainly recognize day and night and pay some attention to the phases of the moon. They would be able to say something about past time, such as "When I was a child," or "When my father was a child," and something about future time, such as "When my child grows up." The time in between might be counted by tides or changing winds or snows, but these old, known ways might or might not be adaptable in the climate of the island. Only the immediate rhythm of day and night and the waxing and waning of the moon—which occur everywhere—and the marking of passing time as human beings are born, grow up, and die are known to all peoples.

Every known people have some idea about how a group of families should live together, about who should give the signal to go hunting or fishing and who should start a religious ceremony. Every people have some way of acting in groups, to clear ground, to give feasts, to hunt together, or to mourn the dead. But there are very great differences in the kinds of organization they would know enough to arrange. For example, there are some very simple peoples who build one house for all the members of a group to sleep in, and there are others who build separate shelters for each family. Some peoples always do things together, but among others each man hunts or fishes for himself. The only thing we can be sure of is that they would know that human beings must live in groups, that one family is not enough for living a full human life. So, although one family might start over again, they would live and act as if there were more people, keeping alive the memory and hoping for the day when there would again be several families.

We know too that they would have some ideas about making life more beautiful, as by ornamenting the body; ornamenting their tools or weapons; drawing designs on the ground or carving the bark of a tree; using their bodies to make pleasant, special movements; patterning sound by singing, or beating on the ground, or blowing on pipes or reeds, or twanging a piece of gut or sinew. The idea of art and the idea of music would be there, but we cannot be certain what forms these ideas would take.

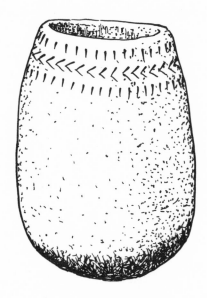

Finally, our castaways, whatever the level of culture and wherever in the world they came from, would have some interest in explaining their existence in the world and some idea of how they might influence the powers they believed to preside over the world. We can be sure that they would have some ideas about life and death, good luck and bad luck, and about illness, and some belief that man by taking thought can do something—make presents, utter threats, keep rules, recite special words—to influence those powers above and beyond nature that we call the "supernatural."

These then, when you look them over, are the basic ideas that all men share with one another and that people of any human society on this earth would be able to rely on if they were cast without tools or weapons on a desert island or if they were the only survivors of a catastrophe that had devastated the rest of the earth. They would know about making things—shelters, containers, tools, and weapons—and about using fire; they would have a language; they would have the idea of the family, ideas of property and privacy and of the need for rules about sex and the care of children; ideas about doing things in groups; ideas about ornamentation and about patterning movement and sound; and they would have some beliefs about supernatural forces in the world.

These ideas, because they are shared by all living peoples, can be said to be as firmly the inheritance of the human race as are those things which we do not learn but inherit biologically from our ancestors. Ideas that are shared by only part of the human race—writing, mathematics, methods of tempering steel, systems of law or politics—are not yet safely part of our inheritance. They could be entirely lost by the destruction of all the people who know about them and of all the books and buildings and machines in which these ideas are now preserved. If there were buried ruins of civilization, then some day the descendants of the very much simpler people who had survived *might* develop a kind of civilization that would make it possible for them to guess what our engineers' designs for radar meant. But this is only a possibility. We can be certain only that man has for as long as he wants to keep them those ideas and inventions that all men share. If we want any particular idea—such as writing—to be safe from destruction, then we must be sure that every people in the world know about it. Only when this is so is an invention safely a part of our human inheritance.

Old Questions and Different Answers

WHEN we look at the basic inventions which are shared by all the peoples of the world from New York and London to the most remote valley in the middle of New Guinea, we find that although they seem very simple they are all things which it took a long time to invent—perhaps half a million years, perhaps longer. Much of the slowly accumulating knowledge on which all culture is based was acquired by forms of man who lived on earth before the appearance of *Homo sapiens,* the form of man to which all the peoples of the present-day world belong. Paleontologists, the scientists who study prehistoric forms of life, have worked out what some of these earlier forms of man were like. But as yet there have not been enough exploration and digging in Africa, Asia, or Europe for scientists to fill in all the links, and we may never have enough information to reconstruct just what kind of family life or tribal organization earlier forms of

254

men had. However, from the records left by hard materials—human and animal skeletons, pottery, stone tools, paintings on the walls of caves—we can build up part of the story.

When we think about the past we can also apply what we found out as we used the knowledge we have of peoples now living and tried to see what any group on earth know about if they had to make a fresh start. For these are all things about which human beings must have known as they spread out over the earth, pushing farther and farther into remote places—into the high mountains, into the jungles, out to the little flat, hurricane-swept islands in the Pacific Ocean—looking for somewhere to live. Sometimes they must have moved in search of places where game and water, roots and berries, were more plentiful. Sometimes they must have moved away from places which seemed unsafe; for although they would not have known, for instance, that the mosquitoes which carry malaria breed in swamps, they might have moved away from a place where too many people sickened and died. Sometimes they must have been pushed back by other peoples who wanted their land, or wanted to enslave them, or tried to convert them.

Anthropologists think that the Americas were peopled by migrants who crossed Bering Strait—not all at once but over a long period of time—and that descendants of the migrants reached Patagonia, in southern South America, some five thousand years ago. How long ago migrants crossed to the Americas can in part be judged by the absence in the New World of a number of inventions which are widely distributed in the Old World. When Europeans discovered the Americas, such things as the use of the wheel, the true arch, and plow agriculture were still unknown on the two American continents. Though it is possible that chance voyagers may have crossed the Pacific and landed on the west coast of the Americas, scholars at present think that the high civilizations of the New World must have developed independently of the high civilizations of the Old World.

This means that the builders in the great civilizations in Middle America and in the Andean region of South America had to invent all the methods of architecture and engineering which they used in making roads and irrigation systems and fortresses and pyramids and palaces. The peoples of the New World made pottery which in the quality of the clay, the glazes used to make the pots waterproof, and the beauty of the shapes and the painted designs is as fine as Old World pottery. But because they never got the idea of the potter's wheel, all this pottery was made by hand. In weaving, however, the peoples of Peru developed every fineness of thread and every type of stitch known in the Old World, so it can be said that they developed independently the art of making cloth.

Border designs from Peruvian ponchos

Domesticated animals native to the Western Hemisphere

There is no sign that the peoples who came to the Americas had any domesticated animal except the dog. You will remember that although northern peoples of the Old World herded reindeer, the Eskimo only hunted the wild herds. The turkey was domesticated in Mexico, and in the Andean region llamas, alpacas, and guinea pigs were domesticated; other than these, no creatures were taken over by men in this way in the New World, and no people got the idea of milking an animal. If we consider what ideas about domestication a people might have who had only dogs, these are: An animal can live dependent upon human care, no longer responsible for its own food or self-protection; an animal can help a human being by hunting, carrying, or watching; an animal can be raised to provide meat; an animal's skin or hair can be used to make things; an animal can be a plaything or pet. All these ideas were developed in different parts of the New World, but with very few elaborations. The plow was unknown in the New World; it can be used only where there are domesticated animals strong enough to pull it, such as oxen, water buffalo, or horses.

Agriculture, based on New World plants, seems to have been invented independently in the New World. Among the most important plants grown there were maize, or Indian corn, beans and squash and pumpkins, manioc (in the tropics), potatoes (in the South American highlands), and cotton. After the discovery of America, New World plants—maize, manioc, potatoes, tomatoes, tobacco, peanuts, pineapples, cacao, and many others—spread all over the known world. Some plants, like maize and potatoes and manioc, have become basic in the diets of other peoples; some, like coca (a plant cultivated by South American highland Indians for medicinal use), have given us useful medicines; some, like cacao, which is now the principal crop in Ghana, are the basis of prosperity in other lands.

So, for thousands of years the peoples of the New World worked with a very old set of ideas which had been brought from Asia; and these peoples developed their own high civilizations in which people lived in great cities built of stone, had irrigated valleys, roads, fortresses, systems of communication, taxes, and complex political systems, and accumulated knowledge. But even so, they were curiously lacking in inventions long taken for granted in the Old World. When we compare the ancient high civilizations of the Old and the New worlds, we can see some of the relationships of later ideas to earlier ones; and we can realize how precious each invention is, for we can never be certain that it will ever be made a second time. In the New World, although the whorl was used for spinning thread and various peoples used the whirling action of the bow drill to make fire or to drill holes, and (in Mexico) an attempt was made to put wheels on miniature objects, no New World people ever really got the idea of the wheel,

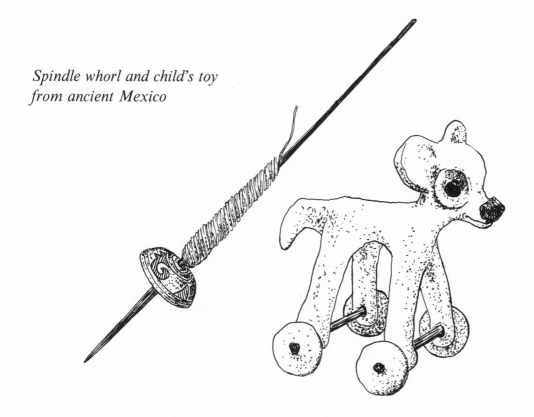

Spindle whorl and child's toy from ancient Mexico

which is necessary for drawing any sizable load overland, for putting to use wind and water power in water wheels and windmills, for speeding up the making of pots, and for making machines that depend on rotating parts.

Thinking about our castaways, we saw the things that have been learned and have become as much the possession of all human beings as is their biological inheritance. However, there is another way we can look at the history of man. For instead of bringing together the inventions shared by all men everywhere, we can arrange in a sequence all the inventions which have ever been made anywhere and which are now part of our modern cultural inheritance. We can place at one end the knowledge of the simplest Pygmy tribes and at the other the laboratories and libraries of a great university; we can compare an atomic-powered submarine with a birch-bark canoe or the crew of a jet plane zooming over the mountains of New Guinea with the savage down below who is toiling up a mountainside, limited to his own strength in what he can carry or move. If we put things into a sequence of this kind, it appears that there is something in human culture which ensures that men will gain more and more control over nature and will find more ways of drawing energy from nature. We get a feeling that each old invention is replaced by a new and better one. It seems clear to us that at any one time in man's history there was somewhere on earth a best—a most efficient—way of traveling on land or sea, under the sea or in the air, a best way of sending information from one place to another and of storing what men knew. It seems clear also that when a better way was invented, human beings naturally followed it. This is how most Americans feel about the world, for we are accustomed to seeing old models replaced by new ones; still, living men have watched the first flying machines develop into jet planes and have seen how cotton and silk were replaced first by rayon and later by nylon and dacron and other artificial fibers. So Americans are surprised when they come upon people in other countries who go on using old forms of plumbing or appear to be satisfied not to use any plumbing at all.

Yet in general it is true that a "better" way of doing a mechanical task—transporting a heavy object, sending a message, manufacturing something—will replace the less efficient way of doing it. But it is true only if we limit ourselves to those inventions which are concerned with power and energy, with doing things more quickly, more cheaply, or more simply, or with turning out more efficient products.

We can think of man moving from the use of bone and wood and stone and shell to the use of ground and polished stone and then to the use of metals—gold, tin, copper, bronze, iron, tempered steel, and modern alloys (mixed metals). From a time when

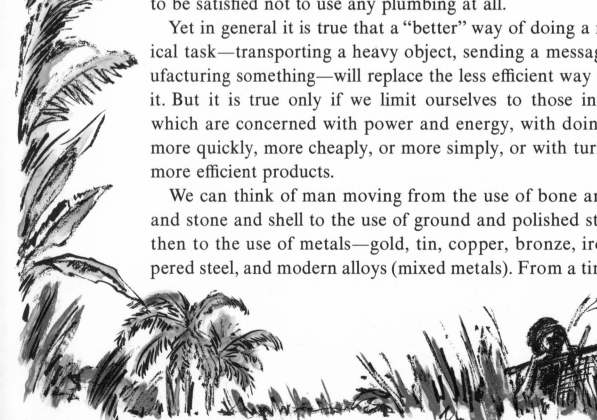

man's main energy was supplied by his own back and arms and legs, we can think of a time when energy was supplied by animal power—horses and donkeys, dogs, oxen and camels, reindeer and llamas—and later by wind and water power, and still more recently by machines which, by burning wood and coal and oil, tap the stored energy laid down in the earth, until now we are learning also to use atomic energy and energy drawn from the sun. Or we can see how man has progressed from a stage when languages were only spoken and no records were kept; to a stage when he could use bundles of sticks to make winter counts, or knotted ropes to help him remember how many items had been counted or what the parts of a message were, or pictures to give the idea of a story or a message; to a stage when man got the idea that a picture could always stand for the same idea or a kind of mark for the same sound, and then he could begin to write.

If we make sequences of this kind, we will notice that all great civilizations made or used these inventions in some form. It was necessary to have sources of energy, and so before machine power was invented, great bodies of men were brought together to build stone monuments like the Egyptian pyramids or the palace at Knossos. It was necessary to keep records and to send information from one part of an empire to another by means of human beings, as the Ashanti did; by means of roads along which human messengers traveled, as did the Incas, who built an empire but had no writing; or by means of writing, as the Romans did. Looking back at the procession of great empires we can also see, as if in a procession, new methods of organizing people, of communicating information, and of using energy. And looking at the modern world we can see how millions of people are tied together not only by writing and by rapid travel but also by the power of a human voice transmitted by radio, as in World War II when Churchill rallied all the people of England to stand firm against the Germans. If we compare past and present, we can see a tremendous contrast between an empire in which mes-

sages were carried by running men who, as they fell exhausted, passed along the words to fresh runners and a modern country in which people thousands of miles apart can talk to each other by telephone and whose ambassadors, traveling by jet plane, can go to the ends of the earth in a few hours. Yet we can also see that back of ancient and modern countries there lies the idea of living in something like a nation. It was this idea that the forest-living Ashanti worked with as they built up their chiefdoms and their nation centering on the golden stool in Kumasi; and it is this idea that a new country like Indonesia, of which Bali is now a part, is working with. This is the idea that many peoples can be grouped together—can act together, speak a common language, and have one law—in one country in which all men can travel and trade and make their homes, all equally safe from attack.

When we look at man's history, we can see how great civilizations grew up from simple beginnings; how, even without the inventions which made any one civilization great, the idea of civilization itself could spread; and since the invention of writing how almost no important ideas have been lost. In a way, we can think of each of these civilizations as if it was a messenger running along the road of world history, handing on, as it fell exhausted, its knowledge of how to make tools and weapons, ships and wheels, armies and navies, taxes and law courts. Following only one small strand, we can see that the Mycenaeans learned from Minoan Crete, and that in turn some of what they knew went on through the Greeks to the Romans and so to France and England, Germany and Italy, Russia and the United States. Some things have been lost along the way, but of the major inventions very few indeed have been lost.

But only if we limit ourselves to those inventions through which man has increased his power to grow food, to bridge rivers, to cross deserts and mountains, to conquer continents, can we build sequences which show that man has learned throughout history to make improvements. If instead we look at other parts of life, those parts which are concerned with men's attempts to understand their place in the universe and to give themselves dignity and nobility through their ways of living, we cannot make comparisons of this kind.

Among the very simplest peoples we find beginnings of ideas about the universe and man's place in it, and so beginnings of that part of philosophy which is called cosmology. Some primitive ideas about the origin of the world and of man are very crude, and we have little difficulty in placing as simple the different ideas thought out by peoples without any history, who knew only the geography of their small part of the world and who knew nothing about the size of the earth or the sun, or about the movements of the planets, or about the age of plants and animals or of the earth itself. When in turn we compare the ideas of primitive men with those of modern astronomers who may be discussing the question of whether the universe as we know it developed gradually or was created in one great explosion, it may at first seem easy to say that the modern discussions are "better." For modern astronomers use much more knowledge and say things in a much more complicated way. Yet, if you think about it a little, you will see that even the most modern astronomer does not in his discussion of *how* the universe came to be, answer questions about *why* the world is here and what man is.

Modern astronomers and geologists and paleontologists and archaeologists can tell us a great deal about how the world has developed, but as yet we have no way of measuring how one view of man's *spiritual* place in the world is better than another. The religions which we call the "great religions" are those with a view of man which many different peoples can understand and accept. They are the religions which are hospitable to every human being.

And especially they are religions which have inspired devoted missionaries to go out to bring other people into their religious faith. As the great religions spread across the world, the little religions which belong only to one tribe or one people yielded to larger ones which give more people room to believe in and to serve the same deity. In this sense we can talk about "great religions." But if we try to measure the religious faith of a Plains Indian fasting in the wilderness, waiting for his guardian spirit to speak to him, against the religious faith of a member of a world-wide religion, there is no way for us to measure either one.

When we look at all the different religions which the peoples of the world have developed, we find that certain ideas have appeared over and over again. Sometimes we can trace one idea back through time and show how one people borrowed it from another. There is, for instance, a belief that sorcerers can make people sick by sending small hard objects into their bodies; to cure a sick person, the sorcerer or someone else with special powers has to remove the object, a stone or a crystal or a bone, and show it to the invalid and his relatives. Today we would regard this as no more than a magician's trick. But for the people who practiced this form of healing, the whole thing had religious meaning. The stone which the curer concealed in his hand or mouth was simply a way of handling pain, something which could be seen and felt. In some places these stones are even called "pains." This idea is found in so many remote parts of the world that scholars believe it is a very old invention which has been passed on from one people to another.

Another religious practice which has come down through history is the use of blessed water for special purposes—to purify the thing it touches, to remove evil, or simply to bless and purify a person who wishes to pray or who has finished praying. However, the idea that water is pure and can be used in special ways connected with religion is such a natural one for human beings to have when they are trying to get closer to the supernatural world that we believe many different peoples have thought of it. So we do not need to trace all religious uses of water to a single invention somewhere far in the past.

All of the great religions have used some of the same basic ideas—the idea of prayer, the idea of sacrifice, the idea of fasting. All have some idea of a special place for worship. And in all religions we find special individuals who become priests or preachers or healers through training, or through experiences such as trance or vision, or because they themselves have been healed of some great illness. Certain religious ideas seem to be quite natural to human beings living on our earth.

All human beings have a long childhood during which their parents must care for them, feed them, and protect them. The idea of this relationship between parents and children is one which has been woven into many religions and is always there, ready to be used in new ways when a prophet arises to give new life to an old religion. The relationship of the weak and the strong is also found in different forms in prayer. The Plains Indian, fasting in a lonely place, begs the supernatural to take pity on him. In many prayers, God is addressed as a father. But in Bali where people thought of life as a circle, the spirits of the ancestors and the gods themselves were often spoken of as the children of the living people who prayed to them.

The idea of sacrifice, giving up something in order to bring oneself closer to the supernatural world, is a very old one. The sacrifice may be a very solid object—a chicken or a water buffalo or even, in some parts of the world, a human being. Or a man may sacrifice his life—give up his family or all the comforts of ordinary living—and live entirely to serve his god. Or the sacrifice may become very small indeed, a short fast or a few pennies dropped into a collection plate. But the idea is there.

When a small group of primitive people give up their tribal religion and come into a world religion, it is possible for them to do so because they are human beings who have already tried to work out a religious relationship to the universe in which they drew on such common ideas as the sacredness of water and fire, the need for prayer and sacrifice and offerings. But besides this, the world religion may give them the feeling that all men, not just the people of their own village or tribe, are brothers.

Wherever we look in the world we also find behavior for which we use the word "magic." By magical practices, men try to control what happens in the world not by prayer or by altering their own spirits so that they will be more closely in tune with an unseen world, but by charms, or by sets of words which have to be repeated perfectly, or by imitations of whatever they want to have happen. Fairy tales are full of this kind of magic: magical objects like wishing rings and wishing wells and wonderful objects such as Aladdin's lamp which had only to be rubbed to bring

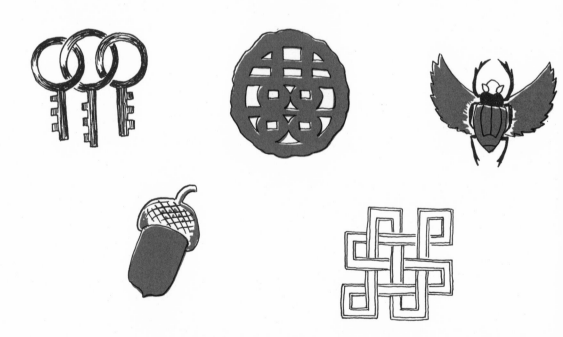

All these symbols, whether ancient or modern, are meant to bring good luck

up an obedient jinni. The main point about magic is that people believed it worked by itself; it did not matter who used it if it was used correctly. Anyone who found or bought or stole the lamp or the stone or the sword, anyone who could learn the exact words or the exact act believed that he could make out-of-the-ordinary things happen—could have good luck at fishing or hunting, start or stop the rain, cause the death of an enemy at a distance, or protect his ship during a storm.

As men have found out more about the natural world, science has taken over many of the things that were once treated magically. Instead of reciting charms, we improve the diet of chickens to get more eggs; instead of wearing talismans, we get immunized or vaccinated to protect ourselves from sickness. But the state of mind which made primitive peoples invent and rely on magic has not entirely disappeared. Just as people once felt helpless in a world they did not understand and tried to control the wind and the rain, the crops and the supply of game, by magical methods, so also today many people feel helpless because so much that happens to them in the big cities where they live seems outside their control or outside their understanding. When a person

hangs a mascot on the dashboard of his car, instead of learning and going by safe driving rules to protect himself from being hit by other cars on a super-highway, he is still trying to use magic to control the behavior of other people. Many people use the new drugs, the antibiotics and sulfa drugs, not for their specific curative properties but as if they were like the magical stones and roots and berries and leaves which men begged or bought from magicians ten thousand years ago.

So while we can say that there has been change in the kind of behavior that is related to magic, the changes that have taken place are not like the ones that took place as men invented better forms of transportation or communication. Many things that once were treated magically are now handled in different ways. But the old ideas have not disappeared; they continue in new forms. Where once people wore specially shaped shells or tiny scraps of cloth covered with mysterious writing, today they look for magic in different places, but they still seek for it.

When we look at the peoples of the world, we also find everywhere the use of taboos. Their use grows out of a third way of thinking about the world, different from the religious way and the magical way. It is a way of thinking that we found in very simple form among the Eskimo. We use the word taboo to mean something which is forbidden, and the idea behind taboos is that if people know exactly what is forbidden and obey the rules about it, they will be safe; but if they break the rules, then automatically —no matter why they did so—some terrible punishment will fall on them. So, for instance, the Eskimo believed that the goddess Sedna, when she created land animals and sea animals, made rules about keeping the two kinds of animals apart. If someone broke these rules, even accidentally, the Eskimo believed that the game would disappear and people would get sick and a whole village might die off. So, too, the Ashanti forbade any mention of an ancestor's misfortune, for they believed that the angry ancestor

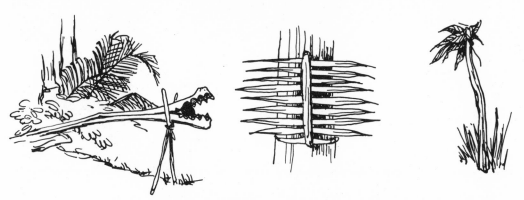

"Taboo" is a word from the South Seas, and all these signs are taboos against picking coconuts. The palm-leaf rib crocodile on the left warns that thieves will be eaten by a crocodile; the bundle of leaves on a stick at right warns a thief that he will be blown out to sea if he steals.

would then punish the person and perhaps his whole family; only in wartime, when a battle was going against the Ashanti, did they deliberately break this taboo so that the ancestors would get more angry and fight harder against the enemy.

Like deep human ideas of trust and help, which are part of religion, and like the ideas based on the human desire to control the world, which are part of magic, ideas about the effectiveness of particular taboos have changed. And yet the idea of taboo itself reappears in many forms. Taboos may be as basic as the universal human prohibition against marriage between parents and children, or they may be concerned with some small detail, such as the prohibition against shouting in a Cheyenne tepee where a medicine bundle was kept. But the idea is the same: If the rule is broken, punishment will follow automatically. Few modern Americans fear the taboo against walking under ladders, but still fewer would test out the taboo against the unluckiness of thirteen.

When we consider man's several ways of thinking about the world—through religion, through magic, and taboo—we find that although particular practices have changed, these ways of thinking continue. And we find, too, that we cannot measure or compare such things as religious faiths.

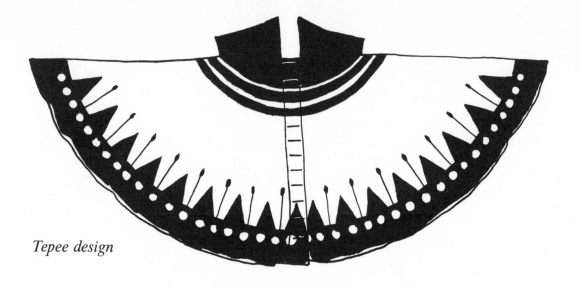

Tepee design

If we now look at the arts through which men have tried to make their lives beautiful and meaningful, we will find that these are also difficult to compare. Of course, we can follow sequences of invention in the arts. We can follow men's ideas as they learned to build in stone and to carve bas reliefs high on the walls of temples or palaces, and we can say that some peoples were greater builders than others or had grander views about what could be done by carvers working with stone. This is a question of scale. Or we can think about music. If we compare a people who had only the simplest instruments—bamboo sticks for beating

Façade of an Indian temple

out rhythms, or flutes with two or three stops—with a modern people whose music may be played by a symphony orchestra, we can see great advances in the making of instruments. But if we try to compare the flute songs of one Indian tribe with those of another, or the music of a Balinese gamelan orchestra with the music of a European orchestra—both complicated, both dependent on the use of complex instruments and on a knowledge of musical scales, on tuning and pitch—again we are left without any measure. Each is a different kind of music, a music which is related to the way in which the people who make it live and feel. We cannot say that one is better than the other, as we *can* say that a wheeled cart is better than a group of slaves with packs on their backs and that a modern truck is better than a horse-drawn cart.

We can, of course, say that one people have done more with one art than they have with another. So, for example, we can say that the Ashanti were less interested in carving and metalwork than some other West African peoples were. But, like many other African peoples, they developed a most intricate and beautiful drum language. Their spoken language depended in part upon tone for its meaning. That is, a sound spoken in a high tone of voice had a different meaning from the same sound spoken in a low tone of voice. Because of this, it was possible by combining two drums, each with a different pitch, to translate the tones and rhythms of words into the tones and rhythms of drum beats, and so to create a poetry of sound, the meaning of which was clear to the trained listener. By means of their drum language, the Ashanti could send messages far across the bush. For instance, this message to take up arms:

Ashanti Porcupines [warriors] seize your powder belts!*

---

*From R. S. Rattray's *Ashanti*, Clarendon Press, Oxford, 1923, p. 256. By permission of the publishers.

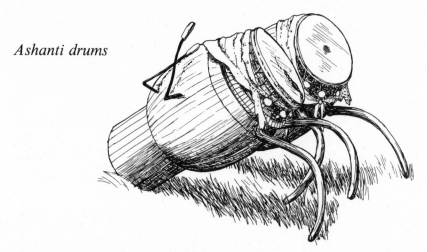
Ashanti drums

Or they could play on their drums the long history of a famous chiefly family or the songs that accompanied ceremonies, from one of which these lines are taken:

> The hero holds a gun and a sword to fight.
> Make yourself arise.
> The leopard is in the thicket.
> The thicket shakes like anything.
> Leopard, walk softly, softly.
> O King, walk softly, softly.*

None of the other peoples we have described made music of this kind, and we can say that the Ashanti and other peoples of West Africa have developed drumming to a special high art.

Whether we think of music or carving or painting or dancing or theater, we can find a place or a time in the long history of a civilization in which a particular art has been cultivated while some or all of the other arts have been neglected. Very occasionally, in what is sometimes called a golden age, many arts are developed at one time, and music and poetry and painting and theater will flourish at once. Such periods we can find in the history of primitive peoples just as we can in the history of Greece or Italy or England. Among a people who carved the decorations for their buildings and their dancers' costumes, artists may

* Rattray, *op. cit.,* p. 208.

become so excited when they get good tools that there may be a burst of new carving and painting and a burst of songs and dances to go with the new carvings. So we can compare one period in a people's history with another in terms of how many of the arts they cared about.

But when we look at the combination of arts or even when we look at one art alone, we cannot find a definite progression. Only if we analyze a whole art form into many parts—as in thinking about music we may divide it technically into kinds of instruments, kinds of scales, types of harmony, sizes of orchestras, thematic complications, and so on—can we make any kind of picture of advance. Similarly, we can analyze Eskimo ivory carvings, Ashanti

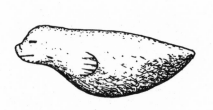

gold weights, and Cretan bead-seals in terms of how the material —ivory or brass or stone—is handled, or of the precision with which tools have been used. Or we can single out and study how a design element, perhaps a dot in a circle, is used and elaborated. Art historians can show how the techniques of an art developed and how one people have borrowed from another, as when Samoans use modern Western designs on their bark cloth, or painters in Paris or New York get ideas from African carving.

In art the thing which we cannot measure or use for comparison is what we call style. Style is what makes an Ashanti gold weight unique, recognizable as the work of an Ashanti artist and no other. Style is also what makes us see the relationship between what a people do with one material and one art form and another; so in Bali we can see how dance is related to temple carvings and to offerings to the gods and to images of the dead. If we look at the work of Minoan artists, we can see that at different periods they learned techniques and even took over ideas of design from other artists in Egypt and Asia. And yet the Minoan style of painting and carving is unique, quite unlike the styles of the peoples whose skills they learned and whose ideas caught their imagination. In this sense, each is incomparable with any other.

It is particularly when we look at the sources of artists' ideas that we can see the difference between the two kinds of invention we have been thinking about. Artists—musicians, painters, danc-

ers, carvers—move freely in time and space, choosing among any ideas known to them those which fit into their own imagination. But once we have developed a modern engine to run a ship, we do not go back to using a primitive paddle or a sail except for fun. For play, like the arts, has variety rather than a sober, steady insistence on efficiency and improvement. And the games of the other peoples, like their arts, remain something to delight the modern world, something in which there can be free exchange from one people to another.

Besides the uniqueness of each art style, because of which we cannot say that one style as a whole is better than another, and besides the artist's freedom of selection through which things

Ruins at Angkor Vat in Cambodia

1. *Chinese embroidered pattern on a dress*

2. *Wool fabric from Egypt, fifth century*

3. *Pattern on a Kirghiz woman's dress*

4. *From a parchment manuscript of the Haggadah. A Hispano-Jewish work dating from the end of the thirteenth century.*

5. *Part view of a small cover from Chinese Turkestan. This is silk embroidery on silk.*

6. *Pattern on an embroidered pillow case from the Ukraine*

7. *Portion of a painted wainscot decorating a private house built in 1603 in Aleppo, Syria*

8. *A tile from Persia, thirteenth century*

1

8

7

All drawings are based on designs in
Ornament in Applied Art, E. Weyhe, 1924

2

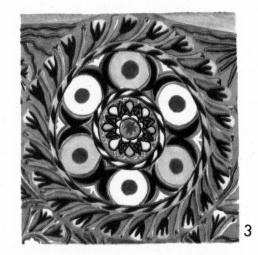

3

A variety of designs

showing

the characteristic style

of different peoples

4

6

5

separated in time and space can be brought together in something that is also altogether new, there is another curious thing about the arts. Once people have developed a style, they seem to tire of it; the very things that once seemed fresh and vivid suddenly seem dull and repetitious. We do not yet know just how this happens. It may be that a style of building a great cathedral or a Mayan pyramid or a giant skyscraper does not satisfy some of the people working in that style as architects or painters or sculptors and some of the onlookers who come to watch and admire, to pray or live, in these great buildings. Or the very people who most cared for a style may be the first to tire of it when they cannot think how to make the spire of a cathedral any more like lace and still build it of stone or how to make the outside of a skyscraper more smooth and functionless than it is. And then they feel that the only thing to do is to make a new beginning. Or change may come about through the people who find that they cannot work in a particular style and are always looking for some other way of making the kind of beauty they want. Or a change in some other part of the culture—the invention of the airplane, or the discovery of a new country, or the invention of a new kind of political system—may make the old style of architecture suddenly seem out of place. Or perhaps it is all of these things together. We do not yet know.

But we do know that although styles do develop and decay, it is not enough to treat them as if they were like living things that are born, mature, and die. Instead we have to look at the part each individual plays in developing a style. So when we think about our skyscraper architecture, we have to include all the individual men and women who design the buildings, pay for them, criticize or applaud them, as well as those who try to build in a different way and those who say, "Look at what they are doing in Sweden," and those who think that skyscrapers are out-of-date because of modern traffic, and those who say, "The thing to do is to spread our cities out flat."

As with the other problems we have been considering in this book, we can best study all the individuals who work at a style by looking at a small primitive society. The things we learn by doing this can give us new ways of understanding what happens in great civilizations. When we do look at arts of different peoples, we find that each has a style that appeals more to some people in *our* society than it does to others. If you look at the designs on pages 278-79, each of which shows the characteristic style of a different people, some will seem to you more beautiful than others. But if you show these designs to your friends and to your parents and to other people, you will find that they will not all agree and will begin to argue in favor of their own choices. Some will think that one style is the most beautiful, and some another. But no one will argue in this way about the greater amount of power that can be provided by a motor as compared with the human arm.

Those of you who are more interested in music can try out the same thing by listening to records of music from different parts of the world. When you have listened to a great many different kinds—Balinese gamelan orchestras, Chinese operas, West African drumming, Eskimo game songs, Spanish gypsy songs, Scottish ballads—you will find that some of this music seems beautiful to you while some of it seems merely strange. And again, other people may or may not agree with your choices.

In some cases, *all* of you may find only ugliness in a piece of music or an art design which another people have found beautiful enough to sing or play or look at over and over again. This comes about because all of you are used to certain styles of music or design and not to others. All of you can follow some of the rhythms and sing some of the tunes that are not too unlike the kind you have learned; other rhythms and tunes may only sound like senseless noise in your ears.

But your individual differences in choices have, we think, another explanation. Some of you know that you would rather look at pictures than listen to music, or the other way about; and, looking at designs, each of you thought some more beautiful than others. These differences between yourself and your friends come about because of differences within each of you that are related both to the different ways you were brought up in your families and to the person each of you is—someone not quite like anyone else.

We have seen that every human culture has been constructed so that everyone in it can live, learn the rules, speak the language, and use the tools and weapons. But no human culture has ever been built which was liked equally and in the same way by every

from *The Lascaux Cave Paintings,* by Fernand Windels,
The Viking Press, Inc., 1950

person who has grown up learning that way of living and seeing the world. It is just these differences in individual taste that make for variety and change. But it is also the uniqueness of each individual, as many different people imagine and think and try their hands at making something, which makes each culture unique as the people who belong in it try to create a satisfying picture of the world.

When we look at all human civilization we can see three processes that are continuously at work. One is the slow sharing of every gain until it belongs to the whole human race, as the idea of the family is shared by all peoples. One is the progressive improvement by one civilization after another of man's ability to use energy and master the world around him, as motor power is replacing the energy supplied by domestic animals and the bare human arm. And one is the succession of different religious and artistic and philosophical forms, each of which has in itself enriched the world and has given place to other forms different from itself and incomparable with it.

The Steps We Know Must Be Taken

FOR the first time in history we know enough about the world we live in, the human beings who inhabit the world, and the conditions under which individuals, families, communities, and nations can live so that we can really look ahead. And when we do, we can see what some of the problems are that must be solved, even though we do not yet know how to solve them.

Our first and most pressing problem is how to do away with warfare as a method of solving conflicts between national groups or between groups within a society who have different views about how the society is to be run. If you look back, you will see that warfare was an invention, just as ways of handling government or taxes are inventions. You will see, too, that once people use an invention they go on using it until they find another which they think is superior.

284

A people living at the level of the Eskimo—in small groups with their energies focused on the problem of survival—had somehow to work out what to do when two strong men in the same group quarreled. There had to be rules about what to do when one man killed another and rules for getting rid of a real troublemaker (as the Eskimo did by killing him when the whole group agreed he was a danger to them). But there was no war, no situation in which the men of one group, acting under a set of rules summed up in a word for warfare, would fight the men of another group.

Once men had invented the idea of a group of fighters, then this was warfare, even though each army consisted of no more than ten Pygmies marching out without any special leaders but with bows and arrows in their hands. With warfare came rules about organized fighting. So, for example, if two groups were at war and members of one group came into the other group except as an attacking army, they would be treated as spies and could be killed. And then it was necessary also to have rules about peaceful meetings, for example, rules of hospitality to protect the stranger. But as the Eskimo did not have the idea of war, so also they did not have the idea of peace, the absence of war.

Among the Plains Indians we saw real warfare. They distinguished between war parties and peaceful visitors and had rules about when a group could go to war and how warriors should behave at home and abroad and rules about the spoils of war—arms and horses and captives. With the Plains organization of warfare went the idea of having peace chiefs and war leaders, of having an organized police group within the camp or tribe, and of having rules about fighting within the group. For as soon as a people have warfare and special weapons intended for use against other human beings—not just spears or hunting knives raised in anger against rivals—it becomes necessary to prevent members of the group from using such weapons against each other.

Though Plains Indians often adopted war captives into their own tribe, they did not have the idea of conquering another tribe in order to make themselves a bigger nation. They did have the idea of voluntary confederation. Among the Blackfoot, several bands would join together in the same tribal ceremony or buffalo hunt, but then each band would go off again. They also had the idea of peaceful alliances, which could be either temporary or more or less permanent. So, for instance, the Blackfoot were perma-

nently at peace with their neighbors, the Sarci, a small tribe who spoke a different language. However, war was a necessity in the kind of world in which the horse-riding, horse-stealing, coup-counting Plains Indians lived and won honor from their fellow men. Without war, there was no way for a man to prove that he was brave and no way for him to acquire large supplies of horses to give away and so prove that he was generous. If one Plains Indian tribe had conquered all the others, their whole way of life would have been altered. On the Plains, when a tribe could no longer fight successfully with the other, the tribe itself retreated from the unequal contest.

However, other American Indians did have the idea of a confederacy designed to keep the peace among a group of tribes who had previously fought each other. The Iroquois Indians of northern New York and eastern Canada formed a league, which at first included five tribes and later six. They also made another important political invention, when they devised a kind of society to which other tribes could be admitted. Their governing body met in a long house, in which there was a place for each tribe; this could be extended at one end to make room for more tribes. Within the long house one law reigned, and this willingness to enforce peace among themselves made them very strong, so strong that they were able to hold the balance of power between the English settlers and the French. After the American Revolution, the Iroquois made a treaty with President George Washington that holds to this day. These Indians are still a separate people, living partly in Canada and partly in the United States, free to come and go as they will. One of the Iroquois tribes, the Mohawk, have become specialists in working on high steel structures and go out from their tribal lands in upper New York State to build great buildings and bridges all over the United States as once they sent war parties and hunting parties abroad in the region of the Great Lakes.

But when the Plains Indians—the Blackfoot, the Cheyenne, and the rest—encountered American settlers, they came up against people who were no longer interested in war as a way of life. In Europe in the seventeenth and eighteenth centuries there were professional soldiers—men who were hired as fighters, like the Hessians who fought for the British against the American colonists. But unlike the Plains Indians, the nations of Europe did not need war in order to give men a chance to act like men. Instead, wars were fought to defend or to acquire territory or because of religious beliefs. So the Christian peoples of Europe fought the Moslems, sent armies to Palestine to free Jerusalem, drove the Arabs out of Spain, and pushed back the Turks when they advanced toward Vienna. In the New World, French and English and Dutch and Swedish and Spanish colonists fought

each other, but each group had the idea of establishing a community in which there would be no further need for warfare. Sometimes the colonists made treaties with the Indians; sometimes they tried to push them out of the way or hoped that they could be wiped out entirely; sometimes, as on the big Spanish estates, they tried to turn them into half-enslaved laborers. As the European settlers moved westward, the Indians, who had no idea how to live without warfare, fought them. But when the Indians were defeated and their old hunting life was ended, their whole culture—as we saw when we looked at the modern Blackfoot and Cheyenne—also changed very deeply.

There are also Indians in the United States who did not go to war at all and found ways of defending themselves by building their villages high up on cliffs and on the tops of plateaus, which we call mesas, where they were safe. These peoples, whom we call the Pueblo Indians, were able to keep up their own way of life much longer than the Plains Indians. Nowadays, through education and other kinds of contacts with Americans, they are gradually becoming more like the Americans around them. However, in the past, keeping up their way of life depended on their ability to resist the attacks of other people, and they became specialists in resistance. So for four hundred years a great deal of their energy went into not becoming Spanish and not becoming American, until they fell further and further behind the world around them and it was harder for them to be proud of their ancient way of life and harder for them to change it.

The Ashanti represent a people who used warfare as a continuous tool for building a nation and for acquiring more land and more people, until the nation became too big and unmanageable and they met adversaries who were better armed than themselves. The Ashanti had more highly developed ideas about justice within the tribe than the American Indians did, as well as more complicated ways of settling difficulties among members of the group, and their ideal was peace. Although they had highly organized armies and took pride in their conquests, warfare was not a way of life. When they were pacified by the British—who also had an ideal of peace but used warfare as a way of enlarging their control over lands and peoples—the Ashanti and the British understood each other quite well. Today Ghana is a nation dedicated to the ideals of peace, but it would still fight if it were attacked. There is always the danger that the people of Ghana might be drawn into a war for some principle which they thought was important, just as the American people were drawn into World War I—not because they had been attacked or were in danger but because the ideas of free government for which we stood were in danger in Europe.

Street scene in Berlin after World War II

In some ways Minoan Crete was a society very much like Britain in the nineteenth century; the people on the island lived in peace and sent traders and colonists abroad. If the Minoans fought sea battles, they did not picture them on carvings or paintings, and we do not know as yet what disaster overtook them in the end. But from the remains of the open towns and open roads and the unfortified palace we get a picture of a people who lived at peace at home. Bali, an island like Crete, had also practically eliminated warfare, but the people were quite helpless before the strength of the invading Dutch.

But instead of looking in detail at warlike and peaceful peoples, we can think about the problem in another way. Looking back over the hundred centuries since our modern species of man has appeared on earth, we can think of all that has happened since small groups of Stone Age men roamed the forests, each group needing many miles of land because their hunting tools were so poor and they had no agriculture and no domestic animals and probably no organized warfare. Then we can see that man has learned how to keep the peace within a larger and larger group until now, in India or China there may be four hundred million people in one's own society whom it is murder to kill. This is a very great achievement, for it means that human beings can now feel that someone who lives half the globe away, whom they have never seen or even heard of, who belongs to a different race and who speaks a different language is still, somehow, a member of their own group—a citizen of their country or a member of their religious faith, someone to be defended and protected. (So in World War II, Americans felt especially badly about dropping the second atom bomb on the Japanese city of Nagasaki, because so many Japanese Christians lived there.) And the idea of adopting the conquered into one's own family or tribe, which we found among the Plains Indians and the Ashanti, has developed into the idea of feeding the millions of people who have been defeated in a modern war and of helping them to rebuild their cities, as we did in Germany and Japan after World War II. Just as the Plains Indians needed warfare in order to have the kind of world in which men could show off as raiders and horse stealers, so we, the people of a modern country like the United States, know that we need other peaceful peoples in the world with whom we can trade and from whom we can get new ideas.

West Berlin street scene in 1957

Very slowly, we have invented ideas for the peaceful organization of society and have developed ways for increasing co-operation which can replace quarrels between individuals, contests between groups, and warfare between large states, until today the whole world is becoming linked together. For now there are regular ways of sending letters to every part of the world, and although the exchange of letters may be interrupted by disaster, by a real war or even by a "cold" war—when letters may be opened or destroyed or lost—the idea of an International Postal

Union exists. So, too, we have worked out international rules for publishing books, rules about ships from one part of the world that enter harbors in other parts of the world, rules for controlling the spread of disease from one country to another, and we have a world court and the idea for some kind of international police to keep peace in the world. And we can think ahead to a day when every human being will be a citizen of the earth who, if he is killed by another citizen, will have been murdered. All these ideas have now been invented.

But, of course, while the groups within which it was wrong to kill and necessary to help others grew bigger the groups of people whom it was right and even noble to hurt and kill in wartime also grew bigger. And our tools for killing—spears, bows and arrows, crossbows, muskets and cannons, heavy artillery, torpedoes carried on submarines and bombs carried on planes, and finally intercontinental missiles with atomic warheads—have steadily become more deadly. So today, when a war might wipe out the whole human race, we need inventions to make warfare impossible.

Our belief that mankind will—or will not—be able to make such inventions depends on how we look at the whole story of mankind. If we look at any one civilization, as Egypt or Minoan Crete, Greece or Rome, we see how a particular group of men lost the ability to defend themselves and keep their own civilization alive. But if we look at the whole of history, we see how mankind has continued. One after another, civilizations have risen and fallen. Through some sixty centuries this did not matter in the *long* run, for even though special groups were wiped out and some knowledge was lost, still the human race was safe. But now it does matter, for in a war all countries—great and small, primitive and modern—are likely to be wiped out at once.

Up to the present, men have not invented a kind of world in which peace in each country is important to all countries and in which each country knows that if it fails to keep the peace, all mankind is endangered. So it is fortunate that the absolute need to solve the problem of war has only come now when the sciences

The development
of weapons
of war

of man are far enough advanced that they can be used to solve problems of organizing society, as other sciences were used to solve problems of traveling on land and on sea and in the air.

The problem of getting rid of war comes first. But our success in doing this depends in part on our being able to solve several other problems at the same time. For only if the peoples of the world care enough about living and think civilization is worth working for, will they have the energy and imagination to make these next inventions. In many parts of the world today millions of people live in poverty, hunger, sickness, and fear. For such people the idea of a quick and noble death, fighting for something—the ancient glory of their country, or the supposed superiority of one religious faith or of one "race" over another, or freedom from colonialism—might still seem preferable to the idea of working at the slower and harder task of finding peaceful solutions.

Korean refugee children

So our second great problem is how to make available to all the peoples of the world the gains already made by the peoples of northern Europe and the British Isles, the United States and Canada. For only in these privileged countries is there today enough education, food, and medical care really to go around. Yet our ideals have grown as our knowledge has increased, and today no one in the world, neither the well-fed nor the hungry, is satisfied while anyone goes hungry anywhere.

The countries which have been moving ahead fast are the ones which were industrialized early, that is, the countries in which people learned to use machines to do the work of human hands. In countries like Great Britain and Belgium and the United States less than a quarter of the people work at growing food, and the rest can concentrate on doing other things—manufacturing clothing and furniture and cars, building houses and roads and bridges and tunnels, teaching and experimenting. But in countries like India and Pakistan almost three quarters of the people are needed just for growing food, and only a small proportion are free to do other things and to think about other problems.

So today there is a great gap between the industrialized countries both in what most people have time to do and what they have time to think about. In the ancient world a ruler had at his command much greater luxury than any of his subjects had. But if you look at the way ordinary people lived in any two countries—for example, ancient Babylon and ancient Egypt—you can see that the differences between what one people and the other could do were not so great. Today this is no longer so. In an industrial country like the United States a family in an ordinary home can draw on more energy to provide themselves with food and water, light and heat and refrigeration, telephones and radios and TV, than was available even to a very rich king in ancient times through the work of hundreds of slaves. But in an unindustrialized country great numbers of people live in what we today regard as terrible poverty. They are barefoot, sick, hungry, and uneducated, all conditions which can be remedied but which are not yet being remedied.

As long as the peoples of the world move ahead at different speeds, the differences between what one people and another can do will become bigger and bigger, until the whole world is

Typical suburban development in the U. S. A.

divided between the haves (nations like ourselves) and the have-nots (nations in which there are too many people and too little land), who have got so far behind that they cannot help themselves and we cannot help them. Today we are beginning to think very seriously about this problem. All sorts of suggestions are being made about ways of improving the situation: for instance, by building atomic-energy factories or finding ways of making use of the sun's energy in countries where there is not enough

Street scene in well-to-do part of Kano, the largest city in Nigeria

coal or oil or water power to support modern industry. But here, too, we are racing against time, trying to make workable plans before too many more millions of people are born into misery.

Then there is a third problem: How are people going to keep informed of all the wonderful new changes that are happening? Among the Eskimo a boy of seven years had begun to learn most of what he needed to know; as he grew up all he needed was practice so that he would become more skilled and better able to use his strength. Plains Indians had the idea of giving their children a picture of the whole of life and of letting them play out much of what they would do seriously in later life; then when they grew up they knew what to expect and had acquired the skills needed for Plains life. In countries in which only a few people learned to read and write, as in Bali, those who learned felt superior while those who did not felt forever inferior and

This Eskimo boy wears a modern cap under his hood, and Balinese school children ride bikes

afraid to express an opinion. Finally, just within the last hundred years, the idea of universal education was invented, the idea that all children—boys and girls, rich and poor, bright and stupid—should go to school and get an "education."

An Eskimo boy learning to build a snow house and to harpoon a seal, Plains Indian children playing at breaking camp and going on war parties, Ashanti children learning proverbs, and our children learning to read and write and do arithmetic all have one thing in common—the idea that once a person is educated, he *is* educated. Of course, for some people education might stop when they were twelve years old, while for others—doctors, for example—it might continue until they were almost thirty. But still for each person a day would come when his "education" would be complete, and he would begin to "live."

Today we are beginning to realize that our world is different

American children at school

Adults learn about a "swimming pool" reactor in India

from the world of the Eskimo hunter not only because our way of living is so much more complicated and so many more people are involved in what we make and do and think. There is also a more important difference. In the modern world we have invented ways of speeding up invention, and people's lives change so fast that a person is born into one kind of world, grows up in another, and by the time his children are growing up, lives in still a different world. This means more than that modern-day children cannot learn all the things they need to know from their parents—as formerly children did among the Eskimo, the Plains Indians, and the Ashanti—or from special teachers who know how to read or compose music or interpret the calendar, as among the Balinese or our own ancestors not so long ago. It means more than that all children have to go to school where there are special teachers to teach them while parents and others are busy doing other things in banks and offices and factories, on farms, and in universities. In fact, it means something much newer and stranger.

It means that education is no longer just for children, or just for young people, or just for people at the beginning of their life. This was true when ways of living changed so slowly that the changes could hardly be noticed from one generation to another. But now changes are coming so fast that even the people who are making the new inventions may know about only some of them. For instance, some people are working on new inventions in automation, that is, creating machines that can push the buttons, pull the levers, and open and shut the valves on other machines so that human beings do not need to pay attention to these details every minute. Others are working on inventions that will give us new kinds of energy, for instance, from the sun. And others are working on new kinds of communication, such as simultaneous interpretation by means of which a group of people listening to a speech can put on earphones and hear it translated while the speaker uses his own language.

A good way of understanding the speed with which things are changing is to talk with a grandparent or someone old enough to be a grandparent or great-grandparent and find out in detail what life was like when grandfather or grandmother was a child. How did the milk come? How did news come before radio and television? How did people get from one place to another? What happened when the baby got diphtheria or scarlet fever? What did partly deaf people do about hearing? How was food kept from spoiling? How was the house lit, and how was it kept warm? Some of you who live in the country will find that you still do some things the way your grandparents did, but from TV and the movies you will know about all the new things that have been discovered. You will realize, too, what it means to the world that men can now telephone from any city to any other city and can fly around the globe in hours.

But most important, you will see that in a world which is changing all the time no one's education is ever complete. This means that in school, children not only have to learn what their parents learned in school, but also have to learn *how to learn*. But as we are just beginning to know how to teach people how to learn something that no one knows yet, this has to be recognized as a new problem which is only partly solved.

Besides learning how to organize the world so that the peoples of the world can work out their difficulties and rivalries without war, and learning how to bring the unindustrialized countries into the world to share in the benefits of modern science and industry, and learning how to bring up people who will be able to go on learning all their lives, there are still other unsolved problems.

There is, for instance, the problem of how to make sure that each human being has a chance to become all that it is possible for him to be in terms of all that we know when he is born. Think what this means. Today most people in the world do not grow as tall or as strong as they might if we could combine what we know about how to feed people with getting the food to them. Having enough food for everyone is necessary first, but besides this there is the question of how much and what kinds of food are best for each child. In a few countries, in the offices of the best pediatricians and in the best well-baby clinics, some children —a very few—are already getting this kind of care. In the United States, we can see the effects of better food and medical care when we find that the sons of Harvard graduates are on the average over an inch taller than their fathers.

This means also that we must protect each child by immunizing him against polio, diphtheria, smallpox, tetanus, and other sicknesses so that no child need grow up crippled, deaf, blind, or scarred by these diseases. Today there are some 9 million lepers in the world, and this is no longer necessary. For each child to have the best chance for good health, we must have supplies of .drugs and enough doctors and nurses to use them correctly; but we must also find ways for people to live so that the spread of disease will be checked.

This brings us to another problem. Once we have used our knowledge of medicine to save the lives of millions of babies who otherwise would have died, new difficulties crop up. Among the children who live, there will be some who have special weaknesses and who need special care and education, and these children also may have special gifts and talents which the human race has never before been able to save. Once we have decided that every child shall have the best possible chance to grow up, it will be necessary to provide each one with the necessary things

—glasses, lessons in lip reading, drugs, and artificial limbs, and physical training—for living a normal life.

Besides these physical and medical things, there are others just as important. From scientific studies that have been made only in the last twenty years, we know that in addition to food and medical care children need love and understanding from the people around them—from adults when they are very small and from adults and people of their own age later. We know that every child needs a family. This means that when some member of a family is missing—a father or a mother, brothers or sisters, or, in some places (as in Ashanti) uncles or aunts or (as among Plains Indians) grandparents—we must invent really good ways for a child to have the warm personal experiences he needs in order to grow up as a member of his society. This is a problem that different peoples have struggled with in many different ways, by having orphanages or boarding schools or by encouraging different kinds of adoption. We are just beginning to know, scientifically, how to care for a motherless baby; but there are all the later years when any particular family may not be like the family people expect to have. And so an uncle or perhaps a teacher or a camp instructor has to take the place of a father. And just as adopted parents can be as satisfactory as real ones, and sometimes more so, other ways can be found of making sure that every child grows up with the people he needs. But a great deal of scientific work must be done before we can know what is needed among each kind of people: among farmers in Kansas, new immigrants from Puerto Rico, fishermen in New England, cotton growers in Alabama, to mention only some people living in the United States. When we start to think of all the peoples in the world and what must be done so that all children can have the close relationships they need, we can see that this is an enormous task.

University students prepare to launch their own experimental two-stage rocket

And today, while we are trying to invent ways of dealing with problems which are not solved but also are not entirely new, man is getting ready to leave this planet for the first time in history—to fly not around the world but away from it. Just as in the last five hundred years men have discovered the whole world—and how big it seemed to them—now we shall begin to explore a larger part of our universe. This exploration is so challenging that perhaps it can provide exactly the condition we need for drawing all the different peoples of the earth together, as once a few tribes learned to band together to live within the same law and to share the same food. Then we will not say "the world" or "the earth" any more, but simply "earth," as once savages learned not to think of themselves as "the people," but as "a people."

In this new time, we shall have to learn in ways that are related to the universe what savage boys had to learn 10,000 years ago—how to be absolutely accurate and absolutely responsible so the fire will not go out or the tribe starve. Today we are already setting up rocket ranges where the young scientists of the future can learn to work safely, responsibly, and with absolute precision on the complex and dangerous experiments on which space travel will depend. Once more we are entering a period in which men will have to give their whole attention to what they are doing and in which the safety of the whole group will depend on men and women who, as boys and girls, learned that life in the twentieth century is like a parachute jump: You have to get it right the first time.

Books for Further Reading

This list is just a beginning—a way of helping you to find more books about anthropology and other peoples. In the first part are some general books and a few on special subjects. In the second part are books about the peoples described here, and also a few others about American Indians. Books of folklore, biographies, stories, and some that describe things you can do are so designated. Some titles are out of print, but most of them can be found in your public library. Starred books (*) are for mature readers.

I

Allen, Agnes, *The Story of Archaeology.* New York, Philosophical Library, 1958.

* Benedict, Ruth, *Patterns of Culture.* Mentor Books, MD89. New York, New American Library, 1946.

Benjamin, Nora, *The First Book of Archaeology.* New York, Watts, 1957.

* Boas, Franz, *Primitive Art.* T25. New York, Dover Publications, 1955.

Burns, William A., *Man and His Tools.* New York, Whittlesey House, McGraw-Hill, 1956.

* Childe, V. Gordon, *Man Makes Himself.* Mentor Books, M64. New York, New American Library, 1951.

* Coon, Carleton S., *The Story of Man.* New York, Knopf, 1954.

Edel, May, *Story of People.* Boston, Little, Brown, 1953.

———, *The Story of Our Ancestors.* Boston, Little, Brown, 1955.

* Fairservis, Walter A., Jr., *The Origins of Oriental Civilization.* Mentor Books, MD251. New York, New American Library, 1959.

Fenton, Carroll Lane, and M. A. Fenton, *The Fossil Book.* Garden City, Doubleday, 1958.

Irwin, Keith Gordon, *The Romance of Writing.* New York, Viking, 1956.

Keesing, Felix M., *Native Peoples of the Pacific World.* New York, Macmillan, 1954.

* Kluckhohn, Clyde, *Mirror for Man.* Premier Books, d58. New York, Fawcett World Library, 1957.

Laird, Helene, and Charlton Laird, *The Tree of Language.* Cleveland and New York, World Publishing, 1957.

* Linton, Ralph, *The Tree of Culture.* Abridged by Adelin Linton. K76. New York, Vintage Books, 1959.

———, and Adelin Linton, *Man's Way from Cave to Skyscraper.* New York, Harper, 1947.

Lisitsky, Gene, *Four Ways of Being Human.* New York, Viking, 1956.

* Pei, Mario, *All About Language.* Philadelphia, Lippincott, 1954.

* Sapir, Edward, *Language.* Harvest Books, HB7. New York, Harcourt, 1921.

Steichen, Edward, *The Family of Man.* Prologue by Carl Sandburg. New York, Museum of Modern Art, 1955.

Underhill, Ruth, *First Came the Family.* New York, Morrow, 1958.

White, Anne Terry, *The First Men in the World.* New York, Random House, 1953.

II

Bali and Indonesia

Courlander, Harold, and Robert Kane, *Kantchil's Lime Pit, and Other Stories from Indonesia.* New York, Harcourt, 1950. (folklore)

* Covarrubias, Miguel, *Island of Bali.* New York, Knopf, 1942.

* McPhee, Colin, *A House in Bali.* New York, Day, 1946.

Crete

* Cottrell, Leonard, *The Bull of Minos.* New York, Rinehart, 1958.

Eskimo and the Arctic

Blackmore, Anauta, *Wild like the Foxes: The True Story of an Eskimo Girl.* New York, Day, 1956. (story)

Freuchen, Peter, *I Sailed with Rasmussen.* Trans. by Arnold Andersen. New York, Messner, 1958. (biography)

* ———, and Finn Salomonsen, *The Arctic Year.* New York, Putnam, 1958.

Freuchen, Pipaluk, *Eskimo Boy.* New York, Lothrop, Lee and Shepard, 1951. (story)

Gillham, Charles E., *Beyond the Clapping Mountains: Eskimo Stories from Alaska.* New York, Macmillan, 1943. (folklore)

Keithahn, Edward L., *Igloo Tales.* Indian Life Readers. United States Indian Service. Lawrence, Kansas, Haskell Institute, 1950. (folklore)

Stefánsson, Evelyn, *Within the Circle: Portrait of the Arctic.* New York, Scribner's, 1945.

Washburne, Heluiz Chandler, and Anauta, *Land of the Good Shadows: The Life Story of Anauta, an Eskimo Woman.* New York, Day, 1940. (autobiography)

———, *Children of the Blizzard.* New York, Day, 1952. (story)

West Africa

Courlander, Harold, and George Herzog, *The Cow-Tail Switch, and Other West African Stories.* New York, Holt, 1947. (folklore)

Courlander, Harold, with Albert Kofi Prempeh, *The Hat-Shaking Dance, and Other Tales from the Gold Coast.* New York, Harcourt, 1957. (folklore)

* Lystad, Robert A., *The Ashanti: A Proud People.* New Brunswick, Rutgers University Press, 1958.

Rattray, R. S., *Akan-Ashanti Folk-Tales.* Oxford, Clarendon Press, 1930. (folklore)

American Indians

Bleeker, Sonia, *The Navajo: Weavers and Silversmiths.* New York, Morrow, 1958. Sonia Bleeker has written many excellent books about the ways of life of American Indians. All these books are published by Morrow.

Catlin, George, *The Boy's Catlin: My Life among the Indians,* ed. Mary Gay Humphreys. New York, Scribner's, 1910.

Cooke, David C., *Fighting Indians of the West.* New York, Dodd, 1954. (biographies)

Dorian, Edith, and W. N. Wilson, *Hokahey! American Indians Then and Now.* New York, Whittlesey House, McGraw-Hill, 1957.

Eastman, Charles A. (Ohiyesa), *Indian Boyhood.* New York, McClure Publishing Co., 1902. (autobiography)

———, *Indian Scout Talks.* Boston, Little, Brown, 1914. (things to do)

Ewers, John C., *The Story of the Blackfeet.* Indian Life and Customs, 6. United States Indian Service. Lawrence, Kansas, Haskell Institute, 1944.

———, *Blackfeet Crafts.* Indian Handcraft, 9. United States Indian Service. Lawrence, Kansas, Haskell Institute, 1945.

Grinnell, George B., *Blackfoot Lodge Tales.* New York, Scribner's, 1903. (folklore)

———, *When Buffalo Ran.* New Haven, Yale University Press, 1920. (autobiography)

*——— , *By Cheyenne Campfires.* New Haven, Yale University Press, 1926. (folklore)

Hogner, Dorothy, *Navajo Winter Nights.* New York, Nelson, 1935. (folklore)

McNeer, May Y., *War Chief of the Seminoles.* New York, Random House, 1954. (biography)

Marriott, Alice, *Indians of the Four Corners.* New York, Crowell, 1952.

———, *Sequoyah: Leader of the Cherokees.* New York, Random House, 1956. (biography)

Mason, Bernard S., *Dances and Stories of the American Indians.* New York, Ronald Press, 1944. (things to do)

———, *The Book of Indian-Crafts and Costumes.* New York, Ronald Press, 1946. (things to do)

Morris, Ann, *Digging in Yucatan.* Garden City, Doubleday, 1931.

———, *Digging in the Southwest.* Garden City, Doubleday, 1933.

Parker, Arthur C. (Gawaso Wanneh), *The Indian How Book.* Garden City, Doubleday, 1927. (things to do)

———, *Skunny Wundy and Other Indian Tales.* Garden City, Doubleday, 1930. (Seneca folklore)

Running, Corinne, *When Coyote Walked the Earth: Indian Tales of the Pacific Northwest.* New York, Holt, 1949. (folklore)

Tunis, Edwin, *Indians.* Cleveland and New York, World Publishing, 1959.

Underhill, Ruth M., *Red Man's America.* Chicago, University of Chicago Press, 1953.

von Hagen, Victor W., *The Sun Kingdom of the Aztecs.* Cleveland and New York, World Publishing, 1958.

SOME SUGGESTIONS FOR MUSIC

There are today several excellent collections of recorded music from different parts of the world. The two series listed here contain a wide variety of primitive and folk music.

The Columbia World Library of Folk and Primitive Music, compiled and edited by Alan Lomax. Columbia Records, New York City.

Ethnic Series, Folkways Records. (Serial Nos. 4000s.) Folkway Records and Service Corporation, New York City.

Sources

The bibliographical references listed here include the principal sources for the chapters in Part Two. Although no references are given for Parts One and Three, some leads for further reading are included in the following section.

ESKIMO

Birket-Smith, Kaj, *The Eskimos.* Trans. by W. E. Calvert, rev. by C. Daryll Forde. New York, Dutton, 1936.

Boas, Franz, "The Central Eskimo," *Bureau of American Ethnology, Sixth Annual Report, 1884–1885.* Washington, 1888, pp. 399–669.

————, "The Eskimo of Baffin Land and Hudson Bay," *Bulletin of the American Museum of Natural History,* XV, Pt. 1. New York, 1901, pp. 1–370.

Canadian Eskimo Art. Ottawa, Queen's Printer and Controller of Stationery, 1957.

Carpenter, Edmund, "Eskimo Space Concepts," *Explorations,* V, 1955, pp. 131–145.

Collins, Henry B., "The Origin and Antiquity of the Eskimo," *Smithsonian Institution Annual Report for 1950.* Washington, 1951, pp. 423–467.

"Eskimos," *Encyclopaedia Britannica,* VIII, 1956, pp. 708–710.

Freuchen, Peter, and Finn Salomonsen, *The Arctic Year.* New York, Putnam, 1958.

Hoebel, E. Adamson, "The Eskimo: Rudimentary Law in a Primitive Anarchy." In *The Law of Primitive Man: A Study in Comparative Legal Dynamics.* Cambridge, Harvard University Press, 1954, pp. 423–467.

Mirsky, Jeannette, *To the North! The Story of Arctic Exploration from Earliest Times to the Present.* New York, Viking, 1934.

"No Upside Down in Eskimo Art," *Explorations,* VIII, 1957, Item 24.

Rasmussen, Knud, *Across Arctic America.* Narrative of the Fifth Thule Expedition. New York, Putnam, 1927.

BLACKFOOT AND CHEYENNE

Alexander, Theron, and Robert Anderson, "Children in a Society under Stress," *Behavioral Science,* II, No. 1, 1957, pp. 46–55.

Anderson, Robert, "The Northern Cheyenne War Mothers," *Anthropological Quarterly,* XXIX (N.S., IV), No. 3, 1956, pp. 82–90.

Ewers, John C., *The Story of the Blackfeet.* Indian Life and Customs, 6. United States Indian Service. Lawrence, Kansas, Haskell Institute, 1944.

————, "The Horse in Blackfoot Culture," *Bureau of American Ethnology Bulletin,* No. 159. Washington, 1955.

————, *The Blackfeet: Raiders on the Northwestern Plains.* Norman, University of Oklahoma Press, 1958.

Goldfrank, Esther, *Changing Configurations in the Social Organization of a Blackfoot Tribe during the Reserve Period (The Blood of Alberta, Canada)*, Monographs of the American Ethnological Society, 8. New York, Augustin, 1945.

Grinnell, George B., *Blackfoot Lodge Tales.* New York, Scribner's, 1903.

————, *The Fighting Cheyennes.* New York, Scribner's, 1915.

————, *When Buffalo Ran.* New Haven, Yale University Press, 1920.

————, *The Cheyenne Indians,* 2 vols. New Haven, Yale University Press, 1923.

————, *By Cheyenne Campfires.* New Haven, Yale University Press, 1926.

Hoebel, E. Adamson, "Comanche, Kiowa and Cheyenne: Plains Indian Law in Development," *The Law of Primitive Man.* Cambridge, Harvard University Press, 1954, pp. 127–176.

Lewis, Oscar, *The Effects of White Contact upon Blackfoot Culture, with Special Reference to the Role of the Fur Trade,* Monographs of the American Ethnological Society, 6. New York, Augustin, 1942.

————, Notes on Blackfoot Economics. MS.

————, Social Structure of the Blackfoot. MS.

Llewellyn, K. N., and E. Adamson Hoebel, *The Cheyenne Way: Conflict and Case Law in Primitive Jurisprudence.* Norman, University of Oklahoma Press, 1941.

Lowie, Robert H., "Plains Indian Age-Societies: Historical and Comparative Summary," *Anthropological Papers of the American Museum of Natural History,* IX, Pt. 13. New York, 1916, pp. 877–1031.

————, *Indians of the Plains.* American Museum of Natural History, Anthropological Handbook, No. 1. New York, McGraw-Hill, 1954.

Mishkin, Bernard, *Rank and Warfare among the Plains Indians,* Monographs of the American Ethnological Society, 3. New York, Augustin, 1940.

Secoy, Frank R., *Changing Military Patterns on the Great Plains,* Monographs of the American Ethnological Society, 21. Locust Valley, N. Y., Augustin, 1953.

Spier, Leslie, "The Sun Dance of the Plains Indians: Its Development and Diffusion," *Anthropological Papers of the American Museum of Natural History,* XVI, Pt. 7. New York, 1921, pp. 453–527.

Steward, Julian H., *The Blackfoot,* 2nd Ed. Berkeley, California: U.S. Department of Agriculture, National Park Service, Field Division of Education, 1934.

Tax, Sol, *Federal Indian Policy and the N. C. A. I.* Washington, National Congress of American Indians, 1957. (pamphlet)

Wissler, Clark, "Material Culture of the Blackfoot Indians," *Anthropological Papers of the American Museum of Natural History,* V, Pt. 1. New York, 1910, pp. 1–175.

————, "The Social Life of the Blackfoot Indians," *Anthropological Papers of the American Museum of Natural History,* VII, Pt. 1. New York, 1911, pp. 1–64.

————, "Societies and Dance Associations of the Blackfoot Indians," *Anthropological Papers of the American Museum of Natural History,* IX, Pt. 4. New York, 1913, pp. 359–460.

———, "Population Changes among the Northern Plains Indians," *Yale University Publications in Anthropology,* I. New Haven, Yale University Press, 1936.

ASHANTI

Bovill, E. W., *The Golden Trade of the Moors.* London, Oxford University Press, 1958.

Bowdich, T. Edward, *Mission from Cape Coast Castle to Ashantee.* London, Murray, 1819.

Busia, K. A., *The Position of Chief in the Modern Political System of Ashanti.* London and New York, Oxford University Press, 1951.

———, "The Ashanti of the Gold Coast." In *African Worlds,* ed. Daryll Forde. London and New York, Oxford University Press, 1954, pp. 190–209.

Fortes, Meyer, "Time and Social Structure: An Ashanti Case Study." In *Social Structure: Studies Presented to A. R. Radcliffe-Brown,* ed. Meyer Fortes. Oxford, Clarendon Press, 1949, pp. 54–84.

———, "Kinship and Marriage among the Ashanti." In *African Systems of Kinship and Marriage,* ed. A. R. Radcliffe-Brown and Daryll Forde. London and New York, Oxford University Press, 1950, pp. 252–284.

Hailey, Lord, "The Gold Coast," *Native Administration in the British African Territories,* Part III: *West Africa: Nigeria, Gold Coast, Sierra Leone, Gambia.* London, His Majesty's Stationery Office, 1951, pp. 189–280.

Hinden, Rita, *Plan for Africa: A Report Prepared for the Colonial Bureau of the Fabian Society.* London, Allen and Unwin, 1941.

Hoebel, E. Adamson, "The Ashanti: Constitutional Monarchy and the Triumph of Public Law," *The Law of Primitive Man.* Cambridge, Harvard University Press, 1954, pp. 211–254.

Information Department, Royal Institute of International Affairs. *Ghana: A Brief Political and Economic Survey.* Chatham House Memorandum. London and New York, Oxford University Press, 1957.

Lystad, Robert A., *The Ashanti: A Proud People.* New Brunswick, Rutgers University Press, 1958.

Rattray, R. S., *Ashanti.* Oxford, Clarendon Press, 1923.

———, *Religion and Art in Ashanti.* Oxford, Clarendon Press, 1927.

———, *Ashanti Law and Constitution.* Oxford, Clarendon Press, 1929.

Wolfson, Freda, Ed. *Pageant of Ghana.* London, Oxford University Press, 1958.

BALI

Bateson, Gregory, and Margaret Mead, *Balinese Character: A Photographic Analysis.* Special Publications of the New York Academy of Sciences, 2. New York, New York Academy of Sciences, 1942.

Belo, Jane, *Bali: Rangda and Barong,* Monographs of the American Ethnological Society, 16. New York, Augustin, 1949.

———, *Bali: Temple Festival,* Monographs of the American Ethnological Society, 22. New York, Augustin, 1953.

————, "Balinese Children's Drawing." In *Childhood in Contemporary Cultures*, Margaret Mead and Martha Wolfenstein, eds. Chicago, Chicago University Press, 1955, pp. 52–69.

McPhee, Colin, *A House in Bali*. New York, Day, 1946.

————, "Children and Music in Bali." In *Childhood in Contemporary Cultures*, Margaret Mead and Martha Wolfenstein, eds., pp. 70–95.

Mead, Margaret, "Strolling Players in the Mountains of Bali," *Natural History*, XLIII, No. 1, 1939, pp. 17–26.

————, "Community Drama, Bali and America," *American Scholar*, II, 1941–1942, pp. 79–88.

————, *Male and Female*. New York, Morrow, 1949.

————, "Children and Ritual in Bali." In *Childhood in Contemporary Cultures*, Margaret Mead and Martha Wolfenstein, eds., pp. 40–51.

————, "Bali in the Market Place of the World," *Proceedings, American Academy of Arts and Letters, National Institute of Arts and Letters*, Ser. II, No. 9, 1959, pp. 286–293.

————, and Frances Cooke Macgregor. *Growth and Culture: A Photographic Analysis*. New York, Putnam, 1951.

CRETE

Bennett, Emmett L., Jr., and A. J. B. Wace, "Tributes to Michael Ventris," *Archaeology*, IX, No. 4, 1956, pp. 279–280.

Childe, V. Gordon, *The Dawn of European Civilization*, 6th Ed. Rev. London, Routledge and Kegan Paul, 1957, pp. 15–47, 57–83.

Cottrell, Leonard, *The Bull of Minos*. New York, Rinehart, 1958.

Evans, Arthur J., *Scripta Minoa*, 2 vols. Oxford, Clarendon Press, 1909.

————, *The Palace of Minos*. 4 vols. London, Macmillan, 1922-1937.

"From Babylon to Crete," *Scientific American*, October, 1957, pp. 58-59.

Hawes, C. H. and H. B., *Crete the Forerunner of Greece*. London and New York, Harper, 1911.

Linton, Ralph, "Crete," *The Tree of Life*. New York, Knopf, 1955, pp. 323–338.

Mylonas, G. E., "Prehistoric Greek Scripts," *Archaeology*, I, No. 3, 1948, pp. 210–220.

————, "Mycenaean Greek and Minoan-Mycenaean Relations," *Archaeology*, IX, No. 4, 1956, pp. 273–279.

Pendlebury, J. D. S., *The Archaeology of Crete*. London, Methuen, 1939.

————, *A Handbook to the Palace of Minos: Knossos with Its Dependencies*. London, Parrish, 1954.

Pope, Maurice, "The Linear A Question," *Antiquity*, XXXII, No. 126, 1958, pp. 97–99.

Ventris, Michael, "King Nestor's Four-Handled Cups, Greek Inventories in the Minoan Script," *Archaeology*, VII, No. 1, 1954, pp. 15–21.

————, and John Chadwick, *Documents in Mycenaean Greek*. Cambridge, Cambridge University Press, 1956.

Index

318 INDEX

About the Author

MARGARET MEAD, Associate Curator of Ethnology at the American Museum of Natural History in New York City, has won world-wide acclaim for her brilliant studies of the primitive peoples of the Pacific. Beginning with her first field trip at the age of twenty-three to Samoa—described in *Coming of Age in Samoa*—she has made nine field trips, and learned seven different primitive languages. She has been principally interested in studying how children and young people learn their cultures, and how these cultures are changing and coming into the modern world.

Honored many times for her outstanding achievements, in 1949 Dr. Mead was elected "Outstanding Woman of the Year in Science" by the Associated Press. She is a member of the Board of Directors of the American Association for the Advancement of Science, a past President of the World Federation for Mental Health, and recently was elected President of the American Anthropological Association.

Her many adult books on anthropology have been widely acclaimed and widely read; this is her first book for young people.